A CROWBAR

IN THE BUDDHIST GARDEN

A CROWBAR

IN THE BUDDHIST GARDEN

STEPHEN REID

thistledown press

Thistledown Press Ltd.
118 — 20th Street West
Saskatoon, Saskatchewan, S7M 0W6
www.thistledownpress.com

Library and Archives Canada Cataloguing in Publication

Reid, Stephen
A crowbar in the Buddhist garden : writing from prison / Stephen Reid.

Also issued in electronic format.
ISBN 978-1-927068-03-8

1. Reid, Stephen. 2. Prisoners' writings, Canadian (English).
3. Prisoners--Canada--Biography. 4. Authors, Canadian (English)--20th century--Biography. I. Title.

PS8585.E606Z47 2012   C813'.54   C2012-904718-X

Cover illustration by Elana Ray/Shutterstock
Cover and book design by Jackie Forrie
Printed and bound in Canada

Canada Council Conseil des Arts   SASKATCHEWAN   Canadian   Patrimoine
for the Arts   du Canada   ARTS BOARD   Heritage   canadien

Thistledown Press gratefully acknowledges the financial assistance of the Canada Council for the Arts, the Saskatchewan Arts Board, and the Government of Canada through the Canada Book Fund for its publishing program.

A CROWBAR

IN THE BUDDHIST GARDEN

For Susan — all the love there is

Kind of faith June has for me, 'bout wore down to nothing
Kind of faith June has for me 'bout wore down to nothing by now
but like the rock in the unfarmed field it's not going anywhere.

— Johnny Cash, as imagined by Michael Blouin

Contents

PROLOGUE
(The Beachcomber)

IF YOU FIND A PINK VIBRATOR washed up on a beach you might laugh and walk on by. But when you find a pink vibrator washed up on a beach and you are in prison — you do a snatch and run.

William Head Institution, a.k.a. "Club Fed," is an eighty-acre windswept rocky peninsula that juts out from the southern tip of Vancouver Island into the Strait of Juan de Fuca. It is both a penitentiary and a place of terrible beauty. At night you can see the lights of Port Angeles, Washington, twenty miles to the south; Victoria, British Columbia, winks from five miles away to the northeast. A high steel fence topped with razor wire and backed up by two gun towers closes off the land entrance, and the cold black waves of the Pacific Northwest lap the perimeter shores like packs of hungry guard dogs.

The prison, as is the nature and purpose of all prisons, serves to keep those of us sent here separate from society, cut off from the daily commerce of life. These craggy shores, dotted with fir and pine, stands of Garry oak, and the twisted limbs of arbutus, has always been a place of forced isolation. In the tribal memory of the Scia'new, People of the Salmon, the local native band upon whose traditional territory the prison sits, this was where, in pre-contact times, those who offended were banished to "find a new direction."

Then from the late 1800s to the middle of the twentieth century, it served as a quarantine station for plague-ridden ships from Europe and the Far East. The lepers were sent to a small offshore island, the victims of cholera and smallpox were confined on this peninsula. Some are buried here. I often think of those who journeyed so far in the holds of sailing ships, in what must have been horrifying conditions: the Chinese, the White Russians, all coming as refugees to the New World. They could only stare across at the lights of Victoria, so close as to seem within reach. They left their bones and their sorrow deep in the soil of this land.

Since the 1950s, when the original prison was built, many thousands of prisoners have passed through the gates here, and this finger of rock and bush has kept us as cut off from humanity as the first native who stole salmon from his neighbour, or the last girl to disembark from the *Empress of Russia*. But times are modern, and the sea that all but surrounds us, especially in the winter storms that batter the rocky headland, also brings in messages, signs of lives being lived out there beyond our reach.

Amongst the plastic shopping bags and Javex bottles, the fishing floats and frayed pieces of dock rope, are flattened Cheerios boxes, empty packages of Hot Blue Corn Chips, a can of Turtle Wax, a baby's car seat, a child's plastic Batmobile with one wheel and the driver missing, a broken piece of plywood with the words FORBIDDEN ZONE.

The detritus up on these rocks sometimes fuels our prison economy. There are men who sit with their faces to the wind, hunkered down out of sight of the patrol trucks, scanning the waves for a bobbing whiskey bottle with a few dregs left or a Ziploc baggy with a few buds of pot, still smokable. One stone alcoholic told me about finding a half-full bottle of Bacardi rum (Black Bat, he called it) and how he downed it on the spot in one gulp. He eventually sobered up and helped found the AA group here, which in a fit of unbridled irony they named The Beachcomber's AA Group.

The dope fiends have to stoop a little lower and look a little harder, combing through the bull kelp and raking their fingers through the stones to uncover the small plastic syringes, which can then be sold for twenty dollars or traded straight for a flap of heroin.

The pink vibrator, once it was rinsed, dried, a couple of new wires soldered in, and batteries installed, hummed to life as good as the day someone walked it out of a love boutique. This buzzing missile ignited a frenzied bidding war. The lucky beachcomber is rumoured to have got twelve bales of tobacco for it and then was able to return and back-tax the buyer for an extra four bales not to reveal his name to the rest of the population.

One young Cree from north of 60 fished out a wallet containing sixteen American one-dollar bills. Functionally illiterate and unfamiliar with the look of US currency, he thought he had hit a jackpot and was downcast when his dealer did the cold math for him. Still, with the exchange rate, he had enough for a flap.

I don't drink or get high these days; my needs are small, and I beachcomb for a different reason. I walk the trails above the coves every day and stare down at the flotsam and jetsam amongst the logs and kelp and natural debris. I watch for that half-submerged square edge, or that colour or texture that is out of pocket with the natural world. I fish out the ripped condom package, a pair of mirrored sunglasses (one lens missing), a high-topped Reebok, size thirteen.

This is my news from the outside world, my mail, posted anonymously and arriving by accident, connecting me to the lives of strangers on the free-side shores. I conjure up the genesis of each item, its journey, its past lives, and try to envision the lives it touched. I imagine a young man on a beach ripping open a red condom package with his teeth, or his girlfriend astride him tearing it open with hers. Could it have been tossed out the porthole of a passing cruise ship after a gay liaison? Did a ten-year-old steal it from his parents' night table to make water balloons and impress his friends?

I wonder about the flattened package of Hot Blue Corn Chips. Was it opened and poured into a bowl at a barbecue? Or were the chips shared by two friends, eaten right out of the package, while they sat on the edge of a dock, their toes touching the water and each other?

Where was the missing Batman for the Batmobile? Who had Turtle waxed their Pontiac Firebird on their day off, then tossed the brown container into the bay? Had the plywood door with the one hanging hinge finally and mysteriously come to rest against the rocks in this place on purpose? In the real Forbidden Zone? These battered and broken and waterlogged objects on the beach are the strings that tie me to the outside world. Each has its story, and it is their stories, unlike my own, that set me free.

THE LAST SCORE

The Last Score

*June 09, 1999, 9:15 am Pacific Standard Time. For me,
emerging from the Shell station toilet, my head rocking from a fresh
jolt of heroin and cocaine, and twenty minutes behind the nine ball,
this am is about to become anything but standard.*

I climb into the passenger side of an old hot-wired Dodge
whose back seat is loaded with enough artillery to light up a small
country. The bank is six blocks away.

We hook a right on the red and head south. The coke is
screaming through my blood but the heroin begins to whisper back
and I settle in a bit, wipe some sweat and scan the traffic. I never
got mangled before a score — not since I was a juvenile throwing
corner stores up in the air.

I take a quick hinge at the toothpick behind the wheel. I
recruited him last night. He has a lint-ball hairdo and the wild eyes
of an amateur. My wheelman and this primer-painted, six-cylinder
scrap of a getaway car have a shared personality: they are both
mutts.

The motor coughs blood, threatens to die, but the tread-bare
tires roll down the sloping pavement and we enter Cook Street
Village, a gentrified hub of small shops and businesses: two cafes,

both with patios, an Italian bistro and an English pub. The village proper is less than three blocks long and on my side of the street it's book-ended by the Royal Bank of Canada and a Mac's Milk. We pass the Mac's Milk.

The sun filters through the leafy canopy of the great horse chestnut and elm trees that line both sides of the street. People sit at sidewalk tables sipping foamy coffees, folded newspapers on their laps. A light breeze trembles the leaves, and their shadows on the sidewalk become like little fishes kissing. A couple strolls by, she with a sweater tied around her waist, hugging him. The whole morning and the people in it seem clear and bright and shiny — everything I'm not. I slide even deeper into the sunless interior of the car.

If ever there was a time to bail it is now, but it's only a fry pan to fire situation. I am ninety grand deep into the crew back East and tomorrow is payday. I have stalled long enough. My only option is to meet their plane. With their loot.

I tug on my gloves and motion Lintball to pass the bank, I need more time. He turns right at the next street and I haul the heavy zippered duffel bag into the front. By the time he has circled the block and is coming up on the rear of the bank again, I have already checked the load on an Ithaca pistol grip 12 gauge pump, have a long-barrelled .22 pistol on the seat beside me and secured a .44 magnum in the holster on my hip. From the back seat, under a blanket, I take a Chinese assault rifle with a square clip of twenty-one steel jacket bullets, each the length of a basketball player's finger. I flick the safety off, cover it again with the blanket. It's a chase gun, one to discourage even the baddest dog from biting our tires.

I rip at the metal fasteners and have my tearaway tracksuit off before Lintball turns into the rear parking lot. He jumps on the brakes; I adjust the eye holes on my clear plastic mask, and exit the still rocking car.

I lope alongside the bank, hugging the red brick wall, the duffel held loosely and my face to the ground hoping I'm incognito in the homemade uniform — a SWAT ball cap and POLICE stencilled boldly on the jacket. But the mask — as I catch my reflection in the bank's glass doors — a product of some last minute shopping, too, with its rouged cheeks and red painted lips, makes me look more like bank robber Barbie than a facsimile cop. I place a gloved hand on the crossbar of the front entrance doors and push inside.

～～～

Three months earlier. Three o'clock in the afternoon, my birthday, March 13th. One of those brilliant champagne days that comes to Victoria in the early spring. Seated at a small ornate table on the raised patio of Café Mocha with a thimble-sized coffee in front of me, I observed the circuit traffic in the Cook Street Village, nursed a sense of detachment, and amused myself by imagining the lives of the passers-by.

A guy two tables down took a pull on his Gauloise; I envied him the thick smoky hit on his lungs and wanted to ask him for one, but I hadn't had a cigarette in almost a year. My life was mostly defined by ex's these days, ex-smoker, ex-con, ex-bank robber, ex-addict. But there was always one shadow I could never seem to turn into an ex — a sense that I am as separate from this world as a switch-blade knife.

The too familiar feeling had descended upon me earlier in the day without invitation or warning. I had been to a lunch, a birthday gathering of six other Pisces poets and writers. Years ago when we all learned that a bunch of us had been born under the same self-contradictory sign, we planned an annual lunch. "The Literary Fish Lunch Bandits" had grown to include two lawyers and a bookseller. Somewhere before dessert and after my third refusal of wine I began to distance from the comfortable humour of my friends. They were animated about their gardens, happy with their ex-partners, and self-deprecating about their publishing successes or their literary prize nominations. They were smart, sensitive, and sensible people. I saw in them, perhaps wrongly, a coherence, an essential wholeness that I lacked.

Since leaving prison twelve years ago I had wanted desperately to build something of my own life, too. But with every task completed, every responsibility met and promise kept, there came — along with a sense of satisfaction and well-being — another unsettling sense that my life was becoming nervously enclosed. Increasingly I felt too far inside, too weatherproofed; I feared I might lose the feel of the rain on my face and the wind in my hair.

I had made my excuses and left the luncheon early and was on my way home when I decided to stop in the Cook Street Village and people watch. An old man shuffled by, his body bent like the drooping ash of a cigarette. He scowled and struck out with his cane as if loathing the ground he walked upon. Was this how it all turned out? You made something of your life and wound up near the end getting mad at a sidewalk?

I abandoned my coffee and started down the steps to the street. A pickup truck booming rock music cruised past. The driver did a double take but didn't slow down. I watched him park a few blocks away, far enough that when he exited the truck I couldn't make out much except leather and jeans. He jaywalked, dodged a few cars and with one last look my way hustled up the steel fire escape on the side of a low apartment building.

My truck was in the same direction as I headed along the sidewalk, stooping to pick a few of last year's chestnuts off the ground. As I straightened up, shaking the chestnuts like dice, I found myself facing, from across the street, an old red brick bank.

I laughed at the whiff of nostalgia, seeing the Lions in navy, blue, and gold mounted on either side of the glass doors to the lobby. The Royal used to be my bank of choice. I had walked through those roaring lions more often than I cared to remember, but a long time ago.

I was fitting the key into the truck door when I heard my name: "Stevie!" I've got two kinds of friends, ones who call me Stephen and those who know me as Stevie. I looked up. The leather and jeans guy from the truck waved wildly from the landing. He was motioning me over and bounding down the steps at the same time. As he came nearer I couldn't quite fish his name out of the memory pool but for sure he was someone I had walked the big yard with. Close up his eyes were glassy and pinned to the nines. He greeted me with that hand slapping faux exuberance of a heroin high: "Great to see you Stevie, me and my old lady watched you on TV . . . channel surfing and there you were. Hey, come on up, I want her to meet you."

And there it was. My conundrum, my Rubik's Cube without the colours. I was in old brain territory; I simply withdrew the key from my truck door and followed him up the fire escape into the building. It wasn't his "old lady" I hungered to meet, but a much whiter, paler lady from my own past.

He knocked, two haircuts and a shave, and we entered a small airless junkie apartment smelling of toadstools and cat urine. A slow-lidded woman in a housecoat bid me be seated on a sagging couch. It seemed the perfect place to unmake my life, just for this afternoon. Just for today.

I smoked the heroin and got a go flap. I stopped twice on the drive home, once to throw up and once to buy a pack of cigarettes. My wife smelled the tobacco on my breath and saw the long-distance holes in my eyes. She retreated to our bedroom, closed the door, and wept. My birthday cake on the table, surrounded by presents, looked even lonelier.

I slept that night on the couch and in the morning said my junkie prayers, *never again Lord*. Within three days I was back in that toadstool apartment; within three weeks, I was injecting five speedballs a day and the number was becoming a vortex.

I emptied my bank account and flew back to Toronto to cuff a shitload of coke from a crew of old friends, major earners known as The Graduates (from the school of hard knocks). I used my reputation as collateral. By the third month my home life was in shreds. I had either shot or fronted the coke out to some gypsy junkies from whom I had no hope of ever being paid. I was ninety grand in debt, payday was looming, and my life was in the toilet. Time to go to the bank.

~·~·~

I'm standing here holding a weapon the length of a Volkswagen and wearing a mask, yet people are just staring, wondering what it is I want. No one is moving. Thankfully, I've been a hold-up guy so long I've learned the words for "On the floor!" in five languages and two dialects — Mandarin and Cantonese, for the casinos.

Today I give the bank customers the lowdown in English. People begin to fold, to lower themselves cautiously to the floor. I step between the sprawled bodies — a familiar scene; the polished floor looks like a swimming pool that has been drained too quickly.

I wave my gun at the moustachioed manager behind a desk in a glass cubicle. He emerges, sleeves rolled up, tie loose. His hands pose surrender but his face wears a confidence not warranted, as if he knows something I don't. But I already know. An alarm button somewhere in the bank has been pushed. That this score was going to be the feature news bulletin on the police radio channel within the first fifteen to twenty seconds was just a bank robbing fact of life.

The manager starts for the floor but I stop him. Just then, another man wearing the same shirt, tie, and rolled up sleeves ensemble scoots out of a back office already down on his butt. I have the moustached manager still standing there showing me his elbows and palms and what I assume to be the assistant manager on his butt on the floor. For a few seconds nothing happens. Then I realize they are waiting for me.

I had never done a bank alone. Usually I just wore the stopwatch and all I had to do was command the floors and doors while my partners cleaned the place out. Finally I click into gear and tell them I want the back door unlocked, the night deposit bags brought out, and the safes opened up. The two managers stare at each other helplessly and like helpless men everywhere they both cry for a woman. "*Helen!*"

The fifty-ish woman rises timidly from the floor. "The safes can't be opened for another hour, the night deposit bags are already gone, and the key to the back door is in the middle office, first drawer on the right. All we have on hand is the cash in this drawer." With that she steps over to a desk behind the counter and begins emptying the drawer of its money. My heart crashes at the sight — a pitiful pile of fives and tens. There sat the hard evidence, the difference between a drug-fuelled fantasy and the reality of a well-planned score.

I still have to get out of here, I know that much. I get the assistant manager off his butt and on to the job of opening the back door. I swing back around to hold sway on the bank then I spot it. The punch line to an old joke: "When is a door not a door? When it's ajar." This jar lead to the room behind the automatic teller machines.

A new plan *ka-chings* into place like three cherries and an anchor. I throw the duffel bag at the manager and tell him what I want. He rolls his eyes and calls, "Helen, I need you to open the machines." He joins Helen-the-Teller and together they head into the loading room. The assistant manager has the back door opened and I catch a fresh jolt of fear — the car is not in sight.

Stacks of tens and twenties are flying into the duffel bag in three-foot lengths but it's taking too long to withdraw and then unload each cassette. I yell for them to hurry, to throw in the whole tray. They do, and out comes moustache, dragging the now bulging duffel bag. I point towards the back door.

The car and my driver are still there, to his credit and my relief. The manager drops the bag into the opened trunk and I thank him. He slams the lid shut and strides back into the bank without so much as a "you're welcome."

All there is left is to scram. A car driven by what appears to be a hundred-year-old elf pulls into the lot and stops bumper to bumper in front of us. Behind her car and across the street stands a cop in her summer uniform — short-sleeved tunic and navy shorts. Her bare legs are planted two feet apart. She and her gun are in a three point stance aimed right at us. "Stop! Right where you are!"

~·~·~

We back off the elf's bumper and fishtail out onto the narrow street nearly sideswiping a line of parked cars. The *thunk* of the bullet never comes. I'm still expecting the shot as we hit the T-section at the end of the block and turn left, out of the line of fire. Lintball accelerates and we tear up two more blocks then lean into a hard right. A very short street, then a left puts us on the perimeter road of Beacon Hill Park.

I'm twisted around and watching the rear window. There is a three-way intersection coming up, a right will put us on a shortcut through the park. Make that without the cops spotting us and we've got a win. I can hear sirens but there is nothing with us yet. We make the turn but before I can even twist back around Lintball hits the brakes so hard I pitch forward into the dash. We are forced into a moving crawl, trapped behind a horse-drawn tourist carriage. Before I can stop him, Lintball cranks the wheel and speeds off down a paved pedestrian and bicycle path. The entrance is marked by a yellow, No Vehicles sign but that seems the least of our worries.

I'm kneeling in the front seat facing back. A cruiser stops broadside at the yellow sign, spots us, and turns in. Fuck, Fuck, Fuck! I snatch the shotgun, wrangle my body halfway out the window and take aim across the roof. It's only bird shot but the blast and the yellow flame spitting from the barrel should be enough to knock a couple of rookies off our tail. Sure enough, the cruiser brakes but before I can say yahoo, a motorcycle cop steers round the cruiser and comes roaring down the lane. I raise the shotgun and fire again. He swerves, re-guns the throttle and keeps coming.

We fly over a narrow stone bridge, pass the duck pond, and the petting zoo. Lintball is again braking hard. My focus shifts. Behind us the motorcycle, lights flashing, crosses the bridge. Ahead are steel posts sunk into the pavement, the space between them too narrow for the car to pass through.

Lintball halts the car just in front of the posts. He has the look of someone who is about to throw in the towel. I put my foot over his and push the gas pedal hard to the floor — all he can do is steer. The metal posts rip both sides of the car and we pop free into a four wheel slide right across a busy intersection. We get righted, find an opening and barrel our way straight down into the heart of the James Bay neighbourhood.

I begin to think that maybe we have lost the motorcycle cop but then I see it, the white bug shield, emergency lights still pulsing from side to side. We start a long dance, us and that lone ranger on his motorbike. We're racing down the street and he's keeping up a calculated pursuit, staying just out of shotgun range but maintaining an unblinking visual. We're flat out, doing eighty maybe ninety clicks an hour, almost flying velocity on a residential street. I'm wedged out the window, the wind whipping my hair, and for one glorious moment, when that shotgun bucks against my shoulder and all four tires lift free of the ground, I am no longer bound to this earth. But we bounce right back down and the motorcycle is still coming on like a bad consequence.

I think of the Beijing howitzer — but killing's not on my agenda. I come up with another plan as we near a sharp, almost ninety degree, curve on Dallas Road. "Round this corner and stop!"

I'm straddling the middle of the road, standing there, shotgun raised in full lock and load. The motorcycle cop accelerates into the curve before he spots me and when he does, he spills. The bike slides out, the front wheel bounces off a concrete barrier and the white-helmeted cop tumbles ass over teakettle down the grass embankment. I get back in the car. Lintball is jumping out of his skin. "You did it, You did it!"

Now we are clear to backtrack to where we planted a fresh car. But right then Lintball turns back into the chase, right towards a posse of cruisers that have been trying desperately to catch up to the action. Before I can get him turned around, an unmarked but unmistakable squad car comes off a side street and he's got our tail. A hundred yards ahead a black and white pulls into a sideways slide, stops: suddenly there's a cop leaning across the hood pointing his pistol straight between my eyes. Lintball brakes, wheels into a driveway. I bail.

I struggle over a high wooden fence and start through someone's backyard, but my body's betraying me, I'm already zigzagging with fatigue, I'm too run down from the months of abuse. I lean against the rough bark of a tree and throw up a pool of phlegm. I see an apartment building, and stagger towards it, the cries of "there he is, there he is," reaching my ears. I'm expecting to catch one between the shoulder blades any second now but I'm so worn out I feel more resignation then terror.

I make the lobby of the apartment building, push through and start knocking, trying door handles all the way, desperate to get inside one of the back-facing apartments. A laundry room, no exit. I open the stairwell door and through the plate glass window I see a cop, revolver drawn, in a crouched run along the side of the building. I'm trapped. All I can think of is an old Victor Mature movie where he plays an animal trainer helping to chase down an escaped circus tiger. He turns to the city cop and says, "When a big cat is trapped, he will climb," and they cut to the tiger bounding up flights of stairs. I start to climb.

I knock on doors on the second floor; 208 opens and I push my way inside. The futility of my predicament floods through me; I slide the shotgun under the couch and find the bathroom so I can wash my face. The bedroom door is open and I see the elderly woman who had answered the door holding the hand of an elderly man under the bed covers. I imagine they are praying.

I return to the living room and sit slumped with the knowledge that my life is over. The couple emerge from the bedroom and introduce themselves as John and Kathy, as if I were some kind of queer guest. Kathy fetches me water — I must have looked thirsty — and John, an old Serbian freedom fighter, rolls me a cigarette.

We could have sat like that forever as far as I was concerned, but we were interrupted by a pounding on the door. Loud voices ordered everyone to vacate the premises.

Kathy and John did as they were told but I stayed put. The police didn't enter, they simply left the door open and lit up the hallway with klieg lights. An hour went by. I could hear them emptying out the apartments all through the building. I knew they were removing any witnesses first. At least I wasn't going to have to suck on my own shotgun.

Waiting for death, I must have nodded off. They were all over me before I could rub the sleep out of my eyes

～～～

The metal food slot on the cell door drops open with a bang and the hollow flushing of stainless steel toilets echoes up and down the hallway, the gut-wrenching sounds of city cells in the morning. I lay my arm across my eyes and try to shut it all out. I am coming down like a Boeing 747.

Late in the morning a phalanx of seasoned officers escort me into a courtroom. I am barefoot and wearing only paper coveralls and forty pounds of chains. They are laughing at me and congratulating one another over the morning's headlines. They are right, I am a clown. I learn I had spent four and a half minutes in the bank, long enough to apply for a loan.

Weeks pass. More court appearances. My wife hires a good lawyer but we both know I can't beat this beef with a bazooka. I plead out and although the judge listens to my junkie alibi he knows what everyone else, including me, knows — that we live in the arena of choices and now I'll have to live with this one.

～～～

I found myself stripped bare, beaten back from hope, and all out of illusions in yet another prison cell like every other prison cell I had lived in.

The media vilified me as the man who had won redemption, then trashed it. The mayor of the city passed out hardware at the cop Oscars. I lay on my bunk, stared at the ceiling and began to think up ways to take myself off the count.

I studied that ceiling until the first snowfall. I had two months until sentencing. That day I swung my feet to the floor and began to pace, hesitantly at first, seven steps in one direction, seven steps back.

A Man They Loved

My hands are broken, my ribs are broken, and I'm dope sick beyond belief, but I know the real pain is in the mail, deeper than broken bones. It's about broken promises, broken hearts, and broken lives. The headlines in the newspapers are as black and bold as gunpowder. *The Jackrabbit Stumbles*: after thirteen years of freedom, thirteen years of a publicly redeemed life, I have gotten myself wired, robbed a bank, shot at policemen, and held two people hostage. A nightmare I can't imagine away or hide from in sleep.

I collapse on my bunk and try to shut out the glare of the twenty-four hour light. Behind my eyelids life has become everything I can't get back.

I'm forty-nine years old, married to one of the most interesting and beautiful women on the planet, and parent to two incredible pieces of magic, Sophie, who is ten, and Charlotte, seventeen. The forfeiture is unbearable. I see a clear plastic laundry bag lying in one corner of my cell. If I could only get it over my head, wind it tight, airtight, at the neck.

I keep the garbage bag clutched in my hand for five days, as I lie fetal, curled around that cavity that others call the centre of their being. I lie down with the pain and I sweat and I weep. Every five minutes I gather enough strength to do it, to place that bag over my head, and every five minutes and one second I gather enough strength not to do it.

By the weekend I can sit up. Another inmate brings me a plate of congealed stew with a biscuit. I manage to swallow a few plastic forkfuls of the stew, but I don't manage for long. I charge for the toilet bowel and sell a Buick all over the corner of my cell.

The guy who brought me my dinner also helps me change clothes and clean up. That evening I sit on the edge of my bunk, sip a cup of water, and this time keep the biscuit down. I glance over at the plastic bag, now filled with sweaty socks and underwear. Who'd want to be sticking their head into that?

Susan visits. She's been here on previous days but this is our first contact; I couldn't get up to see her the other times. I measure the two guards assigned to escort me to the visiting area. The top of my head comes level with the epaulets on their cannon ball shoulders. I step carefully. I know I am in 'roid country; nobody grows that big eating homemade bread.

They place me in a security booth and it is all Susan and I can do just to sit there, so numb and so saddened, and watch each other weep through that scratched-up sheet of plexiglass. And when we pick up those black forty-five pound telephones and hold them to our ears, all we can do is listen to that weeping until the hour has passed and the guards come for me.

Susan begins to visit every day. Our words come slowly, the trembling of my face, of my hands, lessens. Soon thereafter my lawyer, a good and kind friend, begins to show up for a series of consultations. Each time he comes I am led out to the interview room, and he is waiting, yellow legal pad in one hand, pen in the other, poised to take notes. Just the facts, ma'am. With my bones back in my body, my will to live barely restored, it is already time for me to help him to form a narrative of the crime, to gain an understanding of the facts. Good luck.

As I walk through it with him, recollecting the carnage, it is the faces that emerge most clearly. Bank employees, unfortunate customers, the innocent bystander, the elderly couple in their apartment: the fright in their eyes, the bewildered expressions. And finally, the masked and goggled Emergency Response Team. I didn't ever see the actual faces of the ERT officers, but their feet left a lasting impression.

~~~

In the years prior to my arrest I had been both a volunteer and a paid worker in an area of what's commonly referred to as Restorative Justice. I had served on numerous boards of directors for organizations such as the John Howard Society, LINC, B.C., Prison Arts Foundation, PEN Canada, Spirit of the People, and *Journal of Prisoners on Prisons*. I lectured to crime students, taught creative writing in prisons, and conducted victim empowerment workshops. I was a paid contract worker for Corrections Canada (I had Advanced Security Clearance), helping long-term offenders find their way back into the community. I'd prepared pre-sentence reports, moved prisoner's wives into low-cost housing, driven their children to visits. I was an assistant at parole hearings, I refereed diversion programs for young offenders, moderated victim reconciliation sessions, and participated in healing circles.

In the latter three forums the victim and the offender are brought together in an informal and neutral setting. The objective is to establish a moral relationship between the offender and the offence and to meet the needs of the victims. These sessions were where healing could begin to take place for the parties in conflict. It was an approach to criminal justice wherein anger, shame, and hurt could be transformed into fairness, generosity, and accountability. It was sometimes a way through the anger and the hate. It was often the beginning of hope.

One particular session left a clear impression on my mind. It was not the sad tale of addiction and violation that was unfolding before me — these were all too common — but as I sat there, comfortable in my own chair, a witness to the human clumsiness that passed between this victim and this offender, I experienced a sense of liberation. I felt confident that I would be forever beyond the sad and humbling awkward ritual of accountability. I was so sure in that moment that I would never again be brought before the brass rail, made to stand, and be confronted by my own criminal failure.

And hey, look at me now, I can't even meet the eyes of my lawyer, my friend.

~~~

He writes it all down. He turns the pages as I peel off layer after fresh layer and sink deeper into the territory of my crime. It is like collaborating on a book: I draw images, he writes the text. Early in the draft I think — why couldn't I have been an alcoholic instead of a doper? At least an alcoholic is blessed with blackouts and memory losses. But a cocaine psychosis is nothing short of a chilling distillate; it was as if I had memorized a Quentin Tarantino movie.

The queer part is that "me" — the "I" in the parade of events as they happened — had little or no emotional memory. Cocaine, in a full-blown psychosis, causes an utterly pure detachment. The moral relationship, ironically and sadly, belongs to the person I am this day. The moral compass, the remorse and the shame, are present in me through memory, through me reliving, reattaching myself to the events of that day. Unlike an insane person, I am responsible for my condition and unlike a psychopath I can attain an authentic sense of responsibility.

Still, I wish there existed a meat cleaver I could simply hand to some sort of metaphysical butcher who could lop off the part of me that committed these crimes, and who could send that part off packing to the stoney lonesome. Then the rest of me — the other ninety-nine percent — the part that is a devoted father, a decent neighbour, a dedicated husband, and a caring, useful member of my community could go home.

But it doesn't work that way, and even if it did, who would choose what to cut? A psychiatrist might want my brain for analysis, a tribunal of judges would chop off my hands, the police I shot at, would, for sure, be clamouring for my oysters. And what about the heart? The heart of a parent? That overly mortgaged muscle? Would they drive a stake through it and then return it to my family?

But no, none of this will happen: it's all up on the block and it's all going. In criminal law, and much of life, we are our behaviour. I've offended wholly and I will pay wholly. The nature of this offence calls for a life bid, or at least enough years to pass as a lifetime. I know from experience that the calendar days of those years will march over me like an army of ants, each taking a uniform bite and carrying it down into the dark. But sympathy is not what I am looking for, even from myself. I have earned my incarceration. I just wish it weren't so.

~·~·~

From jump street I had told my lawyer to enter "an offer of account-ability." On November 29th we had what was termed a "mini-trial" in regards to "specific" intent to attempt murder. Three of the charges were dismissed, reduced to careless and criminal intent; one attempted murder stuck.

Sentencing is set for December 20th. The Crown is asking for twenty years, my lawyer will ask for fourteen years — my original "offer of accountability". Neither option feels much like Merry Christmas.

This year my friend Patrick is putting up our tree; Tim is stringing the outside lights; Dano is buying my children's gifts for me; Michael and Marilyn are walking my family through Butchart's Gardens to see the Christmas lights. My mother-in-law isn't making her annual batch of Nanaimo bars and is worried no one will finish up the yams at our family Christmas dinner. My older daughter wants to leave for Mexico or L.A. — just to be anywhere but here for the first Christmas. My younger daughter seems more hope-filled. She tells me on the phone, "It'll get better, Dad, as more Christmases go by, but we'll still go through phases, you know." She is a wise young girl who has learned to separate what her dad has done from who her dad is, something even her dad has yet to learn. When she visits, which is every Monday night at six-thirty, I watch her through the plexiglass as she draws pictures on a pad the guard has given her. She draws me, or my pop cans, lifting her eyes only occasionally. I watch as she carries her art over to the visiting area supervisor, as a present, and I see a ten-year-old girl who will be walking up to receive her high school diploma before I'm eligible for parole. Yes, there will be a lot of phases. I ordered the book she is reading, *Island of the Blue Dolphin*, so we can have our own private book club. I watch her favourite TV shows — *I, Too* and *Sabrina the Young Witch*. She is filling a time capsule for me with stickers and art and letters. She wants to buy me Christmas presents and save them all up for me to open when I come home.

My older daughter, who will graduate from high school this year, is also under the legal visiting age and has to visit me with Susan or with her boyfriend. She puts her arm around her mother's shoulder in court and holds her up in the hallways on particularly trying days. She answers the phone and fends off the media. She makes dinner when Susan visits me in the evenings, or takes her sister to a movie when Susan needs an empty house. I watch her support whoever needs it, including me. Charlotte seems the strongest of the four of us but the crime is, at seventeen she shouldn't have to be.

During the last stage of my sentencing hearing, good friends and good neighbours got up on the witness stand: most swore on the Holy Book, and they all described a man they loved, a stranger to the events described during the trial stage of my hearing. That process was characterized by a *National Post* columnist as a eulogy. Everyone should be afforded the privilege I had to hear the love of friends before his funeral.

My wife was the last witness of the day, and in her trademark grace and humour she described the pain and the joy of our thirteen-year marriage, and I loved her all the harder.

Both children have insisted on appearing on my behalf. I reacted with an emphatic *no* — they've been through enough — but as in most things with children, a compromise was struck. They have each made a video.

All that is left of the sentencing hearing is to see these videos and listen to the testimony of BC's chief forensic psychiatrist. I have read Dr. Lohrasbe's report. He says I empathize and have understanding of the impact of my actions on the victims of my offence. He judges my remorse to be genuine. He's right. He also expresses the opinion that an extended period of sexual interference from my childhood is a significant factor in my life-long battle with addiction. Whether or not he's right, we both agree it's not an excuse for criminal behaviour. But it may give me a handle, something to hold on to, a place to begin again in my quest to become whole. I am determined to go wherever I have to go, to take it as deep as it is deep, to do whatever it is I have to do to become whole, to never commit another offence, to never again get addicted. To become, finally and forever, the man my many friends and family described that day from the witness box.

My previous incarceration lasted fourteen and a half years. Most of my adult life has been spent in some of the toughest maximum security prisons here and in America. Many of those years were spent in solitary confinement. When I think back to those endless days of silence, lying there curled around that emptiness, it at least made sense then. It was designed that way: alone in a cell, separate from all that's human, I was supposed to feel alone. But years after my release, a release I had worked so hard towards, changed so much to accomplish, standing in the middle of a room with my family, that emptiness would return. I felt so inhumanely alone, and it felt so unfair. Surrounded by the people I loved and who obviously loved me, the emptiness didn't make sense anymore.

No human being lives in any state close to constant grace. I had moments when grace visited. It came unexpectedly, and remained ever so briefly. Sometimes, when I produced my life and inhabited it fully, like early in the morning, up witnessing the dawn and hearing the first bird clearing its throat, or over a candle-lit dinner watching Susan drink slowly, the legs of a red, red wine reflecting the flame between us: these times I would be in awe of the world.

These are the moments that as I learn once more to meditate and make prayer, I hope will return for a visit.

This morning, when the judge drops his gavel, my chin will probably be on my chest, and as I so often do when I stand alone and afraid, I will probably be rocking my body back and forth. But I hope that as his arithmetic reaches my ears I will be tilting forward, and thus follow through, begin a new fall, this time towards grace.

Celebrating Midnight 1999–2000

THE JUDGE GAVE ME EIGHTEEN CHRISTMASES. What could be worse than spending Christmas in a county jail? On Boxing Day they tossed my cell and seized the broken-off tip of an Xacto blade. It was beginning to look like New Year's in the hole.

I considered protesting — that my "contraband", the size of a microchip, would make an unworthy weapon, or that one of his officers had given it to me so I could cut my horoscope from a newspaper — but decided to hold my mud. After seven months on a regular unit with too many nineteen-year-old garden gnome thieves listening to Metallica and watching *Judge Judy*, the thought of a little solitary seemed too appealing to risk losing.

What to pack for the digger? Bruce Powe once addressed a Writers' Union AGM, and one phrase had stuck with me: "the future of solitude is reading." My future was a lock. I'd better pack the reading.

I knew they always allowed one book in the hole, the Bible, so I chose *The Poisonwood Bible* by Barbara Kingsolver. King James, Kingsolver, they'd never notice.

A battery of guards marched me down to Segregation — ten cells along a narrow hallway in the basement of the jail. My bed ran across the back of the cell — four inches of concrete topped with an inch thick vinyl mattress. I've slept on futons that were more comfortable.

I tapped on the wall, a three and one. A three and one back. Other wall, no answer. Morse code it wasn't but I knew I had one friendly down here.

A few days later I was kicked back, two thirds into *The Poisonwood Bible* and smoking three a day, compliments of my friend next door. Kingsolver's *Bible* was a providential choice, a story of such unbearable radiance, I rationed my daily pages. New Year's Eve count was down to about four hours and I'd accepted being a quiet witness to the new millennium.

The door to Seg buzzed open and a spitting, yelling, kicking skinny little kid was dragged into our solitude. They wrestled him into a cell: a one-man riot, he pounded his door with his fists, screamed abuse, continually flushed his toilet, and pushed his cell alarm.

Shift change came at eleven, but the kid didn't give up. Unless a prisoner is in danger of harming himself, most guards will ignore the abuse, write him up, and let fatigue take its course. The early shift guard was one of those, but the kid wasn't jailwise enough to spot his replacement.

I opened my book and tried to return to the story of a white missionary, his wife, and four daughters trapped in a jungle of their own. But then the door to Seg buzzed open and the Cell Extraction team swept in. I couldn't see them, but I didn't need to — the army of the dark empire, in black padded uniforms, visored helmets, high boots and Plexiglas shields — like the casting call to a *Star Wars* flic.

"Throw out your weapons! Lay down on the floor and you won't be hurt!"

What weapons? Spit out his tongue? The kid had a roll of toilet paper and a blanket in there.

The team charged in holding up shields and spraying mace. In the end the subdued youngster was carted out hog-tied, to an Observation cell. The hall became very quiet. The outside world would soon be celebrating midnight 2000.

I heard a tap on the wall, dropped to my belly and peered out under the door. My friend next door was using a tightly-rolled newspaper to manoeuvre a fresh-lit cigarette over to me — it was just out of reach. I tore off enough toilet paper to twist into a foot-long string, and tried to fish the cigarette into my cell. First flick, missed. Again, just about; third flick lucky. The string had looped a neat circle around the smouldering cigarette: I was the roping champion of Tobacco Rodeo!

As I began tugging gently, a pair of black boots planted themselves on both sides of that smoke. Pinched! A frozen moment, then one boot lifted and kicked the cigarette in under my door. The sound of footsteps fell away down the hall.

I sat on my little bed, hugging my knees, and took a long hard pull off that cigarette. Some backyard fireworks boomed in the distance and the light reflected in my cell. It was the best cigarette I've ever smoked, but, like solitude, there's never enough. I flicked the butt into my toilet, tapped a three and one on the wall, and escaped to the Africa of Kingsolver's imagination, where all human commerce is both cruel and tender.

And knowing that each day, even one spent in solitary confinement on the dawning of a new millennium, is not an unfortunate gift.

The Last Jesus I Know Of

I'M RIDING THE BENCH OPPOSITE A GUY who tells me he has a spider up his ass. In the other cage, by himself, is a delicately built native with Lola Falana bangs and 34 B-cup breasts poking out of a grey standard issue T-shirt. He/she has fresh gauze dressing wrapped around both wrists and has been talking non-stop dingbat since we scooped her from the infirmary. I hear motors engaging and a long meshed gate sliding open. The Corrections Services transfer van lurches forward and we enter the sally port of the Regional Psychiatric Centre.

Prison is about waiting. The guy with the spider up his ass does his quietly, chin resting in cupped hands, long hair falling like bad string over his face. But Raven — she insists on being referred to as a woman — waits for no man, dives right into her story. They just don't get me. I'm no drag queen, I'm a transgender. A work-in-progress. Do you know how much money nip and tuck operations, botox treatment, silicon, and collagen injections cost? I do. And after all that they refuse to give me the surgical procedure. Then they go, "Oh Raven, why are you slashing up?" Like get a brain, dude!

Raven's vagina monologues are starting to make my teeth hurt. I'm more interested in the guy opposite me. But before I can begin to coax it out of him — the story not the spider — the van pulls forward and parks in front of Admissions and Discharge.

Raven is taken out first. She minces and gingers to the amusement of her escorts. The rear doors open and I start to slide along the bench, my leg chains scraping the dimpled steel floor panels, but the waiting officer holds up one palm and motions the Spider Man forward. The doors slam shut again. I am left in the semi-darkness with no other story than my own.

At the age of fifty, I'm facing the front end of a fresh eighteen-year sentence.

In the dictionary escape is at best "a temporary relief from circumstances." In trying to figure out how to pass the next eighteen years, I discovered the Intensive Therapy Violent Offender Program, a gruelling horror show in which sixteen of the most dangerous offenders are culled from seven regional prisons and forced to endure a year of masochistic and humiliating psychodynamic therapy. I volunteered.

～～～

I'm carrying a new bedroll and a whole lot of apprehension towards a two-storey cellblock, which from the air would look a lot like the Pentagon, only smaller, with one wing missing. This is the world of VHF radios, handcuffs, and fear, not the safest of therapeutic environments. I have pictures in my head of dungeons filled with men screaming or sobbing on their knees — somewhere between Jerry Springer and the Inquisition.

The door to the main dome area opens and the pitch of madness hits my ears. Once considered dangerous and unstable, the men here, who walk as if their arms have been stapled to their sides, have been chemically shackled. Everything that was violent, and all that was human, seems now absent in them. My escort urges me up the stairs where I'm to be housed separately, on the second floor, the Programs Wing.

Upstairs appears eerily quiet; the cell doors have been left hanging open as if there had been some sort of hurried evacuation. The door to the cleaner's closet bangs wide and out pops a kid who looks more like he should be mowing his parents' lawn than mopping a prison floor.

The youngster abandons his mop and morphs into an overeager one-man welcome wagon. His name is D, short for what I don't ask, but when I offer my hand, his face turns crimson. His hand goes reluctantly into my grip, boney, and deformed in the shape of a lobster claw. He quickly tucks it back behind him in a habit as practised as it is tender.

D gives me the lowdown — the other guys that make up our group, I'm the last to arrive, my cell second from the end, anything I need just ask, and oh by the way, could I score him some tobacco from the commissary?

My cell is the same as the countless others I have inhabited over the years — bunk, desk, toilet, and a razor wire view. By the time I have the corners of my blanket tucked in I learn that D is doing a life minimum seven sentence behind a manslaughter conviction while he was still a juvenile. Hence his request — he's asked me to boot for him because he isn't old enough to buy cigarettes.

I know I will eventually have to acclimatize myself to this new-wave-new-age-crack criminal-television-talk-show mentality that encourages the outpouring of explicit and personal details at such breakneck speed. But who wants to hear about a wrecked childhood, a girlfriend's fetishes, or a homicidal act from a person five minutes after you've learned he even exists on the same planet?

In D's case it's forgivable: he's young, nervous, scared, and even though he hasn't said it yet I know he's seen me on the six o'clock news. I'm his idea of a major criminal; for him making Number

One on a Most Wanted list is analogous to winning on *American Idol*. The fact that I feel more busted than brazen won't faze D much; like most young people he is more interested in his idea of a person than the human reality. I leave the tier to get his cigarettes.

Coming out of the commissary I catch sight of D going into the laundry room and give him the sign for the come-and-get-it. I don't make it another fifty paces down the strip before I am confronted by a correctional officer wearing black leather gloves. His jaw juts out dramatically; I want to tell him that he shaves really, really well but instead I answer his question about what was in the bag I just handed off to the kid. Jack Foote — it's on his tag — reminds me we are in a maximum security psychiatric facility and he'll brook no bullcrap on his watch. He knows exactly who I am and says I won't be getting any special treatment around here. Which really means I will be getting special treatment. His belt radio erupts into static, then a few bursts of a language only people in uniforms can understand. It's for me — I'm wanted up in psych assessment for intake testing.

Upstairs in the program area, a middle-aged woman in a track suit ushers me through a doorway marked Assessment Clinic. I feel I have entered a scene in *A Clockwork Orange*. Christina, who is the programs clerk, places a blue file folder and three golf pencils on the table in front of me. She explains these tests will determine my risk factors, measure anger quotients, and help identify my crime cycles.

Most of the tests are short and I begin to rack them up. On a scale of one to five, one being Does Not Apply and five being That's Me To The Nines, circle your choice to each of the following statements. (A) When I become angry I throw things. (B) I like to watch fires. Etcetera etcetera. Essentially they are asking you to admit you are a lunatic.

~·~·~

I am the first to arrive at our group's introductory psycho-dynamic therapy session. The same *Clockwork Orange* room, but no table, nor trace of Christina. The group begins to drift in, filling the thinly padded chairs arranged along the walls. Although I've had glimpses, this is my first opportunity to scope my fellow thugs en masse. No real surprises. A few mullet cuts, three shaved heads, a ponytail, another braided, an oiled pompadour — lots of macho body language.

Most everyone in the room is either quiet or having bus stop conversations with the person(s) closest to them. It's all filler while we wait for a staff member to arrive. *No way am I doing any of that psycho drama shit. I hear the blonde facilitator is a bitch. I don't give a rat's ass. If you give the croaker here a story, it's easy to get sleepers. I ain't never getting out anyway. Maybe it's white to show up the blood when I coldcock one of these cocksuckers. I'm up for parole almost right after we finish.* The trick is not to talk too much, but not to be too quiet either.

Our two facilitators appear and everything goes still. The young woman points first to one corner where the walls and the ceiling meet, and then to the other. Her partner, an earthy looking guy with a bald pate, has his hands in both pockets while he rocks on his heels. By now every thug in the room is trying to recall what he said to the person sitting next to him in the last twenty minutes. There's a tiny camera lens peeking out from each corner.

Alyssa, blonde and white, introduces herself. The affable looking Teal speaks with an authority that belies his appearance. "On paper you guys stink. I have read every one of your files and I wouldn't want you living in my neighborhood. You have all made a lot of bad choices in your lives. We're here to change that. And we hope you are too."

Alyssa, in perfect tag team fashion says, "This program is based in REBT, rational emotive behaviour therapy. It is about identifying the relationship between your thoughts, your feelings, and your behaviour. Can anyone tell me how they are feeling right now? How about you? Yes, you."

I must have been smirking out of the side of my face because I realize too late it is me she has transfixed in those fierce blue eyes. All I can come up with is, "Those cameras make me feel like I've been ambushed."

"Wrong! Firstly no one can make you feel anything. Secondly, being ambushed is not a feeling, you probably feel angry or resentful. We will get into identifying our feelings later, for now I want all you men to remember this — you choose to feel the way you do."

Teal breaks in to tell us how the program is structured. "For now you will go back to your cell and write a life autobiography. It can be as long or as short as you like. You have the rest of the week to finish it."

The guy sitting near the door — I'm pretty sure it's Buster Longines, a genuine hardcase out of Ontario — rises to his full five foot, five inches, stretches, and says, "I don't give a rat's ass what he wants, I'm going to the weight pit." Buster's a thoroughbred alpha male, a prison wheel that's done a gang of hole time. He ambles out the door like an aging fireplug.

Alyssa beckons to me. "We need to talk to you, we haven't done your initial treatment team meeting yet."

Teal bids me to stay seated. "Two things," he begins, "We don't think you were entirely straightforward in your answers, which is common in self-reporting tests. Also, the program psychologist has read your file and diagnosed you with an antisocial personality disorder."

Nothing gets by these guys. My file is only filled with thirty years of robberies, heroin, and mayhem.

Morgan, an older con who wears a wooden cross around the neck, is hanging out with D near my cell door. They are looking for some writerly advice on how to get their autobiographies started. "Keep the pencil moving," is all I can tell them. I head down to the library to sign out a book on Rational Emotive Behaviour Therapy.

For most of the men in our group, serving time kindles a singular construct; for them the world is the thing they stand on. But between these shelves, amongst living books, the shape of your world can shift a thousand times, once for each title, or be changed forever in a single page. In its own way, the prison library is more dangerous than the big yard.

At the end of the row, in a blind corner, I almost trip over Raven, kneeling between the legs of a pink-skinned guy sprawled across an armchair. I recognize him from group — the Duke — a lightweight with a mullet cut. I want to ask Raven what they did with the Spider Man but I can see she's got her mouth full.

I keep moving. After the reality of catching Raven in honeysuckle heaven I need some other worldly self-help, even poetry. I spend a half hour pouring over books on crystals and angels, guides for the twelve different stairways to heaven, recipes for dharma cookies, and chicken soup for everyone but the chickens. Books to help you recover everything from your inner predator to your authentic self.

On the way to the door I nudge out a slim volume by Rilke. The librarian with a huge frown on her face is staring at a *Maxim* magazine centerfold. "All these faces they've been . . . interfered with. Women, men, even the dogs. They've all been . . . " She shows me the magazine. Someone has been doing eyeball surgery with a razor blade.

Outside the library I almost bump into Raven again. This time she appears to be on the losing end of a heated exchange with the Duke. Her lower lip is trembling. "Men," she says before spinning in her elevated loafers and clomping off in her exaggerated way.

"Raven!" I call after her, "What did they do with the Spider Man?"

"He's in the big yard," she throws back, her ass still chewing bubble gum down the strip.

The Spider Man is lying on his belly in the outfield of the ball diamond, absorbed in a patch of grass six inches from his face. I flop down next to him. An ant teeters by. Eventually I have to ask how he suitcased a spider.

"I cut off a cigar tube and put him inside it. Someone's got to look after the little guys, don't you think? They were going to spray paint my cell when I left."

"Does he have a name?"

"You mean like a daddy long legs or a wolf spider or what not?"

"No, I mean like Itsy Bitsy or Norman. Like a name."

Spider Man looks at me as if I'm the one who's nuts. "He's a spider for godsake." Then he falls quiet for a while before adding, "but I think he's the last Jesus I know of."

Back on the tier I close my door and go on deadlock, I'd had enough for the day. I try reading Rilke, I pace, I lie down to sleep but there's too much bad mail being opened. Finally, I go to my desk, take a yellow legal pad from my drawer.

I don't try to capital-W Write. I push me out of the way and write from the first realm of thought. The pages begin to fly, the pencil literally pushing through the paper. I seize on to the memory of a time long buried and withheld from grief. All night, black letters pour on to yellow paper and I write out those things no child should ever have been made to know.

When my head comes up, and I set the pencil down, the sun is climbing over the razor wire. I lie on my bunk and watch the shadows of the bars fall across my body, fragmenting my self. I stare up at the ceiling and, like Rilke, let the past break out in my heart.

~·~·~

Monday, back in group, I do a quick survey and count only fifteen heads. Before I can ask who is missing, Morgan throws up his hand and volunteers to present his autobiography. For two hours, in a matter-of-fact tone, he describes never knowing his parents, the brutal foster homes, a runaway adolescence, a skid row adulthood, culminating in this current offence, a triple homicide — the details of which he is told to save for our next — our crime biography — phase.

Next up is a biker named Vance who was raised on the back of a Harley, left on the doorstep of an alcoholic aunt after his Dad met up with a semi pulling out on to a prairie road. He joined a gang at sixteen and at the age of thirty-two has been a full time criminal for more than half his life.

D informs me that evening that the nervous guy with the acne scarred face was caught by The Foote last night — in his cell, wolfing back a bowl full of paper eyes — so they moved him to downstairs.

Over the next few weeks we stay in this same pattern. One person presents their story each day; no one has to be Sigmund Freud to figure out these were men who grew so tired of being wounded, they went out and wounded something else.

My turn to share my scribblings from my own night of the long knives, and I do so in as steady a voice as I can muster. It is the first time I have spoken these things out loud, and it leaves me feeling fragile, less than certain I have done the right thing.

Buster shows up on the last day of the life bios with a page and a half that is as poignant as it is brief. It is the tale of a kid, who at the age of nine, leaves the front gate unlatched and the family dog gets hit by a car. For three days, as a "lesson", Buster is made to lie in a shallow earthen pit under the house with the body of his pet. With weekends and days off it's taken a month and a half and all

I have learned so far is, that for a lot of people in this room, their first bad choice was their parents.

Teal claps his hands, tells us all what a great job we have done. Now it's time to return to our cells and begin our crime biographies.

Morgan is again waiting for me at my cell door, fingering his cross with great distress. He wants to know what he should do, go through the motions or be completely honest. I ask him what Jesus would do and he nods, as if I just gave him sage advice.

I close my door and begin to write about my index offence. I draw the word images for a sea of frightened faces inside the bank, describe the cop chase and the ammunition fired, the commandeering of an elderly couple in their apartment. I write down my crimes as uncut documentary, unadorned by story or convenient amnesia. By the grace of God there were no bodies, only shocked victims, in the wake of my violence.

Then I enter the misery of addiction, the betrayal of self, love, and family. I write on up to the moment of my arrest. I know if I leave one memory unscraped, one regret unacknowledged, then it will simply stay as if it were a recurring stuck dream that goes on delivering its inescapable blows.

～～～

We are back in the white room the final morning of our crime biographies. Most of us by now are through presenting. Buster had to default on his because of an alcohol-induced blackout at the time, so we got the antiseptic transcript version of a double attempted murder with a hunting knife. Vance had stumbled his way through a home invasion where he tied a woman to a combination wall safe. D had wept as he recounted killing his best friend with a hammer as the guy slept. When D wiped his tears and thought he was finished, Teal said now tell us why. For a hundred hits of ecstasy and half a pound of weed.

As person after person, day after day, has read aloud, the details have become soul numbing. This is Hollywood unpeeled. Characters who use hammers, kitchen knives, weight bars, baseball bats, tire irons, rocks, and guns. Victims left crawling across linoleum, strangled in duct tape, dragged by the hair into the basement, stuffed in the trunk, or carried, limb by limb, into the woods and burned under a pile of leaves. And just when I think I've heard all I can take, Morgan gets up to read his crime biography.

In a killing spree across northern Alberta, Morgan visits farmhouses the way normal people go to ATMs. They begin as robberies but by the third farm in as many days he shoots a young couple because they resisted. Morgan sets the house on fire unaware two kids are hiding in an upstairs closet. One of them, he learns after his arrest, made it out. But even his arrest doesn't come in time. He's at another farmhouse late the following night and he's got a single occupant on his hands, and she's fighting him hard so he flattens her with a glass ashtray. When he realizes she's probably dead he loads the body in the backseat, drives a few miles down the road, parks, and drags her into a stand of poplars. He goes back to the car for a shovel. Returning, he says, "I can't figure out what came over me, but there she was lying with her dress, like all up around her waist." Morgan stops, his face flushed and lined in anguish. "Afterward, I dug a hole and pushed her into it. Then I started filling it up and that's when she coughed." Morgan buried that woman alive. She was seventy-two years old, coughing out that northern Alberta dirt almost as fast as he was throwing it in.

Morgan is the last to present, and when he finishes no one looks at him. Maybe it is the accumulation of all our carnage, maybe it is the fathomless nature of Morgan's crime, but in that moment I think we all know, as the poet said, that there is nothing one man will not do to another.

Later that evening I find Morgan in the chapel, kneeling on a purple carpet beneath a life-sized icon of Jesus. His hands clasped, praying incoherently, he is incapable of even acknowledging my presence.

Not knowing what else to do I simply stay with him. I sit on a pew and witness as a man quakes and heaves his way down to a final and spent madness. Perhaps there are crimes better left covered by the dirt. The buzzer for count sounds. I take my leave, knowing the guards will find him soon enough.

~·~·~

Alyssa awaits the arrival of the whole group before announcing that Teal has a heart condition and will be taking some time off. In two weeks it will be Christmas break so we will resume in the new year.

The last two weeks have been, anyway, strangely anti-climactic. There have been no outbursts, no throwing of chairs, little that is authentic or meaningful, and no breakthroughs.

There are two reasons. After we lost Morgan, and of course the nervous guy who ate the eyes, everyone became cautious. The remaining apostles entered into a no-risk zone. The second is Buster. Each time one of the younger guys takes a chance and starts with something real, Buster growls him down with, "I don't give a rat's ass what you think." After a hundred promising starts were rubbed out by a rat's ass, it became a joke behind Buster's back. Need to borrow a pencil? I don't give a rat's ass. It's supposed to snow tomorrow. I don't give a rat's ass.

I'm on my way to the big yard when I run into Raven. I ask her how life is without a boyfriend and she tells me she's sworn off relationships; she now plans to focus more on herself. Raven looks like, well, Raven, but her presence seems more substantial. When I ask for an update on Spider Man and Morgan, she tells me Spider is Spider and Morgan is still incoherent and four pointed to the bed in the Chinese cell at the back of A wing.

An old native guy in street clothes and a felt cowboy hat approaches us. Raven introduces me to Cecil Johnny, a native Elder who visits this prison. Cecil says he is building a new lodge here and I'm welcome to attend a sweat. I let him know that I'll think about it; Cecil gives me sweet grass before leaving.

By the time the treatment team meeting rolls around Morgan has gone for tests to the Provincial Mental Hospital at Riverview. Alyssa and Christina tell me they are pleased with my level of participation in group though the psychologist who studies us through the camera has added "some narcissistic traits" to my profile.

I want to diagnose the psychologist as a voyeuristic crank but I leave it there knowing he is, of course, right. What he doesn't know is that I may be the only narcissist in the world with a case of unrequited self-love.

Christmas Eve The Foote shows up with his crew for a surprise shakedown on the tier. They toss our cells, making a mess, then depart going, "Ho Ho Ho." The rest of the holiday season passes with Sally Ann Sunshine Bags, attempted suicides, and dark chocolate.

Teal returns in the new year, noticeably thinner, but the ABC's of REBT are growing old. I already have what I need from this program, I'm just occupying a chair, and like Buster and all the other guys, waiting for graduation day. Still, if I hear one more rat's ass I think I'm going to commit homicide. Then it comes, a response to a youngster's complaint of depression.

Buster is all over him, "I don't give a rat's ass. You sleep all day, watch TV. Never work out. You're not depressed, you're weak." The kid clams up. Buster is about half right on this one but that's hardly the point anymore.

The next morning in group I begin, "I believe the saddest thing I know would be a man in his fifties, my age, who has no sense of humour, has never learned to laugh at himself, and whose power over other people leaves the room when he does." I'm not even looking at Buster, but he and everyone in the room, knows who I'm talking to.

"Nobody here gives a rat's ass what you believe." Buster doesn't backwater, I have to give him that.

Later, I see Buster in the bathroom, both hands on the sink, staring down. I figure I better get this over with so I walk in and tell him not to take it personally. Buster doesn't say anything, I don't know where this is going and I'm worried I've pushed him too hard.

Buster doesn't lift his gaze from the sink when he asks, "They all laugh at me, don't they?"

"They're just scared of you is all. It's chow time. Let's eat." But Buster isn't letting go his grip on the sink.

~·~·~

"We are down to our last few weeks of group, fellas."

Teal's words are ones I'd longed to hear, although group has become not half bad. Buster's still not giving a rat's ass, but now he's saying it in a good way. A few of the guys are making jokes and even Alyssa's eyes have turned a kinder shade of blue. If we're not careful it's liable to get downright warm and fuzzy.

Buster, D, and me take a turn in the big yard. It's the spring equinox. Morgan is back from Riverview. He's walking right ahead of us, a little shaky but on recovery row. D bounds off to do a workout; he has put on about thirty pounds of cut muscle and is going to be all right wherever he goes.

The Spider Man is still lying lost in his grassy world. We come around the corner of the track and Raven is hanging off the gate waving me and Buster in. Cecil Johnny wants our help over on the sweat lodge grounds. We are led to a fenced-in security area behind the hospital. A guard lets us in and snaps the gate shut behind us.

Cecil shows us where he wants the willows to be placed in the ground, how to bend and tie them together with red strips of cloth. Buster loves a project and he's been barking like a straw foreman since we started. I tell him I don't give a rat's ass what piece of red cloth he wants me to hand him next.

Cecil directs us to drape heavy canvas tarpaulins over the skeleton frame, then with everything pulled and tucked to his satisfaction, we sit on the ground exhausted and admire our lodge.

"Want to try a sweat?" Cecil asks, holding out towels towards me and Buster. Buster strips down to his boxers; I follow and we grab pitchforks to help Raven carry the rocks and place them in the pit in the center of the lodge.

Cecil sits at the back of the lodge facing the small doorway as we crawl in on our hands and knees. He directs Raven, "because you are two-spirited, my dear" to sit in the north, to his left, and for me and Buster to take the southern side. We sit cross-legged, facing the glowing rocks. Cecil lights the pipe and then Raven drops the flap down over the doorway plunging us into blackness.

There is the hiss of steam. This is the earth's womb: warm and moist and too dark to see. Cecil the Elder launches into a song as old and far-seeing as the wind.

JUNKIE

Junkie

THE BLOOD BROKE INTO TWO RIVULETS along the smooth skin of my inner forearm. My head sank back into the new leather of the bucket seat and my body went limp. Paul returned the glass syringe to its coffin-like case and dabbed at my arm with a soft white cotton ball. His face swam up to mine, as if to steal a kiss. I felt such a helpless peace I would have kissed him back, had I known how. On that warm Indian summer day in northern Ontario, I had just been given my first taste of morphine. I wouldn't turn twelve until the snow fell and melted again the following spring; by then I would have had a lot more of Paul and a lot more of his morphine. By then, I'd have learned to fix myself.

Paul was everything I was not. He was rich, had elegant features, and graceful hands. He owned a new white Thunderbird convertible. Paul was also a grown man, a doctor, and a pedophile. The morphine, of course, was a prelude.

Something was loosed in me that October day, something beyond blood, beyond my bantam genitals from my jeans. There is a memory so fixed and so perfect that on certain days a part of my brain listens to no other. *The top is down on his Thunderbird, the pale autumn sun warm on my skin. The blood running down my arm is like spilled roses. We are hidden from the road, partway down an old tractor trail in the grass. I am pressed against the rich red leather. Not ten feet away, yellow waxy leaves make their death rattle in the late afternoon breeze. I am in profound awe of the ordinary — the pale sky, the blue spruce tree, the rusty barbed wire fence, those dying yellow leaves. I am high. I am eleven years old and in communion with this world. Wholly innocent, I enter the heart of unknowing.*

For much of the winter that followed I lay face down on the couch in Paul's rec room, with my skinny white arm sticking out from under him, waiting for the next jab. I still lived at home, shared a bed with my brother, and ate my porridge with brown sugar every morning at the crowded kitchen table. I carried myself to school. After dinner, I slung my hockey bag over my shoulder and left the house waving to my mother who thought I was spending my evenings at the rink. I can still see Paul's car, idling with the lights out, waiting for me on the snow-packed road, the plume of the car's exhaust rising in the cold air, a ghostly curtain of white vapour I crossed through each time I went to him.

Day-to-day existence became like an old photograph of my former life, faded and curling in at the edges. My body, once eager to explore every nook and cranny of the world around me, seemed now to resist the smallest of efforts. I went to Paul again and again, trying to get me back, trying to jam me back up my veins. But the more I tried, the more gaping the hole became, until so much had been spilled from me only the morphine seemed to matter. The struggle to stop my boyhood from flowing out changed to a struggle to stem the darkness flooding in — the secret self-loathing that pools in the heart of every junkie.

Paul unzipped my childhood, but it's never been as singular or as uncomplicated as blame. Mine is more than the story of a boy interrupted. It is not what Paul took from me, it is what I kept: the lie that the key to the gates of paradise was a filled syringe. In all the thousands of syringes I've emptied into my arm since then, the only gates that ever opened led to the penitentiary. Yet for most of my adult years I have clung to a deep sense of longing, a desire to return to that moment when the plunger hit bottom and the morphine arrived home for the very first time. I have staggered through a turbulent life, but I've lived that life in the arena of possibilities like everyone else. I have made countless choices along the way, broken my bones on good fortune, vandalized the best of my intentions. I have misappropriated trust, defrauded love, and found — then lost — redemption so many times you'd think I had holes in my pockets, all the while trying desperately to transport myself back to that first taste of radiance, to obliterate the dark winter that followed.

I have quit heroin to become a better thief. I have quit heroin to become a better father, a better husband, a better friend, a better citizen. I have maintained these clean and good intentions for years at a stretch, but I have never stayed quit. It's true of men: we keep our dark secrets, hold to an unflagging belief in our manly self-will. We don't ask for directions to the corner store, and we don't ask for help in our lives. I have always returned to the needle and the spoon with a childish thirst, a self-centred insistence that I can attain utopia. The voice of the addict whispers, "Come this way, it will be different this time. Just this once, what you seek will be here." Ad, from the Latin "toward" or "yes" and dict from the Latin "say". Addicts just say yes.

There is a zen-like irony in the junkie slang "to fix". A shot of heroin doesn't fix anything: heroin only gives shelter to that which is broken. Blaise Pascal, the French philosopher, wrote, "Every action involves risk, possibly loss, all action leads to pain." In plainer terms, "Nobody moves, and nobody gets hurt." Heroin addicts want to stop the world from spinning, to fix a point in time where it is safe — an embryonic state, the place before loss.

There were nine children in our family. One died young. We moved a lot when I was growing up. The houses we rented, like the town, seemed always too small; my mother had too little money to raise too many kids. My father was away much of the time: first the army, then the northern lumber camps, then the mines. When he came home he drank hard with his "chums," and they made the kitchen seem even smaller. I loved my dad fiercely, from the misspelled name he had tattooed on his arm the day I was born to the callouses on his hands. And I believe he loved me back in the only way he knew how. My dad would have killed Paul, but the fury he would have saved for me is what kept the silence.

At thirteen I began riding a yellow bus to the regional high school nineteen miles down Highway 17. At first the school, my new-found circle of friends, seemed glamorous. I attached myself to this fresh and affluent town with zeal, spending as little time as possible at home.

My secret life with Paul got easier. His house — with its plush carpets, art on the walls, a refrigerator rich with food, and not one, but two big, shiny bathrooms — was mere blocks from my new school. I hitchhiked home only to sleep. My dad remained absent in one way or another, and my mom was buried under a pile of laundry. I slipped away to become the ghost of my own boyhood.

Being from my hometown was like being from a bad neighbourhood. I parlayed that image into as much leather-jacket mystique as I could among the sons and daughters of merchants and mill managers. These were boys who worried about their golf scores and wore machine-knitted sweaters over houndstooth slacks. The girls had ponytails and wore Banlon sweaters tucked into plaid skirts. They put pennies in their loafers and Kleenex in their brassieres.

We guzzled mickeys of lemon gin, those boys and me, in the washroom at school dances. I drank to wash down the black beauties and Christmas trees I stole from Paul's bag of tricks. The gin helped kill the taste of him; the uppers quelled the nausea. When the dances ended, I would be fighting outside the New Moon Restaurant or walking one of those plaid-skirted girls home. On the sofas in their parents' living rooms, I kissed those girls too hard then stole their mothers' tranquillizers from the medicine cabinet on my way out the door.

Paul took a vacation to Mexico and returned with glossy poolside pictures and a bag of marijuana. He was growing leery of giving me more morphine and, I think, tiring of me. But nothing could shake my determination to extract more from him. An unspoken blackmail hung in the air between us.

Each time Paul gave me the hard stuff he'd written something in a ledger that he left on the bar. One night, high and curious, I peeked. The ledger turned out to be a mandatory account of narcotic dispensations he was obliged to keep for the RCMP. Paul had been falsely recording every cc of morphine he had given me as injections to his patients.

The next day in class I kept staring at my friend Bobby M, wondering if he knew his mother was dying, afraid he'd find out I'd taken the medicine meant for her. I began to fear that everyone would learn about me and Paul. It was like living with an execution date. I started to fragment. One spring morning I missed the yellow bus. I crossed the asphalt highway and stuck out my thumb to cars heading west.

~~~

I landed on the West Coast three years too early for the Summer of Love. In the dark heart of downtown Vancouver I had instead my first summer of heroin. In those few short months I would learn ninety-nine names for junk and lose the one for love.

Main and Hastings, the Corner: I wasn't there a hot five minutes before a young native guy turned me around so his pal could steal my gym bag. The slim contents must have evoked some feeling of kinship because I hardly had time to notice the bag missing before they were handing it back. The first guy put his fist under my nose and told me they called him Box, because that's what he liked to do.

Box took me for coffee at the Plaza Cafe, where there were tiny holes in the bottom of all the spoons. Box filled me in: the Chinese proprietor drilled his spoons to discourage the dope-fiend clientele from stealing them or using them to cook up in his washroom. The cops kicked the toilet doors off their hinges on a regular basis.

I'd barely had had time to stir my coffee when a character everyone seemed to be waiting for strolled in the door. He wore a green suit, and his hair looked like it had been licked by a cat. Teddy Beaver was a bundle player who oversaw a small network of singles dealers. A bundle, I would learn in the weeks to come, was a package of twenty-five number-five capsules of heroin, triple-tied in a prophylactic called a stall. I also would learn to carry the stall in my mouth, ready to swallow it at the first sign of a roust. In those days, simple possession meant a certain trip to penitentiary.

There was a code on the Corner back then: strangers and children couldn't buy heroin. Ray Charles could see I was no cop, but Teddy wasn't going to be responsible for me being "turned out." Even after I had rolled up my sleeve and showed how Paul had already taken care of that, Teddy said he didn't want me catching a habit on his dope. It didn't matter. Box scored off Teddy, and I was "in the car."

Box scurried back to his flop with me so tight on his tail we made one shadow on the scarred red bricks along the alley. We took the back stairs of the Balmoral Hotel two at a time and hit the one john shared by all the tenants of the second floor. There was a round hole where the lock should have been; I braced my foot against the bottom of the door the way Box showed me and kneeled to "keep six" out the peephole.

Box worked quickly, removing a bent spoon, an eyedropper, and the steel point of a needle he had hidden in the toilet-paper tube. He cooked the dope until the water fried at the edges of the spoon, then sat on the toilet and twisted his shirtsleeve into a knot over his bicep. When the veins jumped up, he held the dropper like a dart and sunk the needle into his arm.

Blood flagged into the dropper, and Box squeezed the bulb. His eyes closed and his body slumped against the toilet tank, the needle still hanging from his arm. I shouted his name. When he wouldn't respond, I started to shake him. Box gradually came around enough to repeat the whole cooking ritual, and this time he sank the needle into my wing.

We spent the remains of the day in his room, sprawled across the sagging bed listening to a scratchy Chet Baker record. My tolerance was low, and I about went to heaven on less than a quarter cap. Box didn't get seasick, but me, I ran to the bathroom and spewed my junkie bile every half hour or so.

I entered the world of Hastings Street with all the zest of a kid joining the carny. Box and I shoplifted meat and sold it to the five o'clock crowd at the Blackstone. We dry-tricked the fags over on Seymour, hustling them for ten bucks with a promise to appear. A ten-dollar bill was known as a sawbuck, the currency of the Corner. It is what the hookers charged; the price of a blow job was tied to the cost of a single cap of heroin. Box and I did whatever it took to go back to the Balmoral and get high.

Teddy Beaver appeared on the Corner every afternoon about three and stood there surveying his kingdom. One day he overheard Box ragging on me about rent. He led me by the elbow to a back booth at the Plaza for a *mano a mano*. I went to work for Teddy. Whenever one of his singles dealers needed to be re-upped, I would make the pickup, then the delivery. I was handling twelve to sixteen bundles a day, 300 to 400 caps, and yet I still couldn't score on my own.

Teddy put me away with a hooker called Kitty, whose old man had, until his court appearance that morning, worked for him. He was now sitting out a deuce-less in Oakalla. I retrieved my gym bag from Box's room and waited at the Plaza for Kitty-Cat to finish her shift. She scored two caps and we hailed a cab, stopping on Davie Street at the all-night pharmacy. KC kissed me to pass me the stall, then clip-clopped inside to grab a new kit — one eyedropper and a number 26 point.

Kitty had a one-bedroom in a six-storey building on Butte. She started apologizing for the messy apartment while we were still in the elevator. Kitty was a serial apologist; she was still saying her sorries through the bedroom door while I rummaged in her kitchen drawers for a spoon. I had cooked up and fixed half a cap before she came out in a housecoat. Kitty stood short in flat-bottomed slippers and was every inch a tender mess. I hesitated when she asked me to cook her up one cap — a cap fix was a major habit, one that would kill most users — but I threw it in the spoon.

Before I got even half the whack into her, Kitty was into an overdose. She turned blue. I wrestled her limp body into a cold shower where she came around slowly. Kitty's ex had been "giving her the Fraser River". It was an old junkie double-cross, which in New York would be called giving somebody the Hudson; in Toronto, Lake Erie. Kitty thought she had a major habit but she had been shooting mostly water while her boyfriend "h.o.'d" the dope for himself.

Kitty and I fell into a routine. We kept vampire hours. Every day we woke to the setting sun, did a jimmy-hix; then she put on her high heels and painted her mouth target-red. I put on my sneakers and we caught a cab to the Corner. She went to work at the Blackstone, me to the Plaza Cafe.

Kitty became the mirror I was afraid to look into. The heroin had us both by the throat, and I watched her skin turn grey, her bones start to jut, and sores develop at the corner of her mouth. We began to resemble the other zombie dope fiends, spiritless, single-minded in our obsession. The search for pleasure devolved into the avoidance of withdrawal. If I went without heroin for more than a few hours my nose would drip and my legs would begin to ache. My quest for utopia had become a ritual of drudgery, the daily grind to maintain a habit.

One night on our way home, after she had scored our dope, Kitty announced she was pregnant. I didn't know how. She turned French tricks exclusively, and I was using four caps a day — for all the erections I ever got, she could have had swallows nesting in her vagina and I wouldn't have known. In the elevator my legs wobbled and I got a bitter taste in my mouth. The alarm bells went off, and I spit out an eight-cap stall as I slid to the floor. True to junkie form, Kitty went for the stall before she tried to help me to my feet. The stall she had forgotten to triple-tie.

I woke in the Vancouver General looking up at the gentle face of a nurse. She was touching the tracks on my arms and crying. I closed my eyes, then snuck out as soon as she left the room. I waited in a blue gown at a bus stop across the street for Kitty to come pick me up in a cab. I sat on that bench, fourteen-years-old and so emptied of feeling I didn't even understand why that nurse had been so sad.

Teddy was a no-show one night, and a minor panic set in until Jerry the German went out to Chilliwack and came back with an o-zee already capped up. The word on the street next day was Teddy had been shot eight times and stuffed down a sewer grate. Rumours flew. Some said it was the Roadrunner, a notoriously vicious cop; others said Teddy had double-doored the Chinese Triads. Whatever the truth, his mother, an old east-end matriarch, spent two days and two nights out in the pouring rain searching, until she came to the one manhole cover she hadn't wanted to find. They say the old lady lifted Teddy's body out by herself.

Kitty scored me the first bundle I could call my own. I began putting out singles from a booth in the White Lunch. One night I was tucking a twenty in my sock, having just sold two caps to Donny-the-Poet, when two harness bulls walked in and pinned him to the floor. Behind them came the Roadrunner. He usually carried a wedge-handled flashlight to pry open the mouth of a reluctant hype, but this time he wasn't in the mood for formalities. When Donny wouldn't spit out the stall, the other two cops held him down while the Roadrunner coolly bent a fork around his own hand and began to dig his way into the Poet's mouth. Before Donny could surrender, his lips were hanging in so many shreds his mouth looked like the entrance to a carwash. On his way out, the Roadrunner told me to sit tight, he'd be back.

I phoned Kitty from San Francisco a few weeks later. She had suffered a miscarriage and was home from the hospital. The Roadrunner had come looking for me and had hung her by the ankles from the balcony. She said when he let go of her all she could think of was how glad she was she hadn't gotten the fifth-floor apartment she'd always wanted. The next time I called, her number was out of service.

I was arrested that fall outside Berkeley with a tobacco pouch full of third-grade marijuana. A judge declared me a juvenile non grata; I was flown to Seattle to await expulsion from the country. On the trip from the airport to King County Jail, in the back of the prison van, a black man tried to force me to masturbate him. We were both cuffed, and my struggles to keep him at bay amused the sheriffs no end.

The next morning an FBI agent drove me to the border crossing and turned me over to Canada Customs and Immigration. They left me unattended in a waiting room, and I bolted. I caught a ride to Vancouver and phoned my Uncle Victor, who wired me enough money to buy a ticket on the first Greyhound bus back to northern Ontario.

My mother hugged me for ten minutes straight, but it was a week before my dad acknowledged my presence in the house. I returned to school, ready to repeat the year I had missed, but my determination began to dissolve in the sea of faces in that grade nine classroom. My small-town values, my human values, had been forever altered. I knew things no fourteen-year-old should have to know. The days of catching snowflakes on my tongue were over.

Within months I was gone again. I got as far as Winnipeg, where I was arrested for shoplifting a leather jacket from the Bay and put in the Public Safety Building. I had a cellblock to myself. For a week I saw only a hand that set a cup of coffee and a muffin on my bars in the morning and coffee and a sandwich at lunch and dinner. Then I was sent home. My mother hugged me; my father ignored me. The ink hadn't dried on my probation papers before I was back out on the highway, my thumb hooked in the general direction of Toronto. Over the next few years, I returned to live with my parents for shorter and shorter periods. Sometimes I was brought home in the back of an OPP cruiser; sometimes I came on my own because I felt too beat-up out there. On one trip home I learned Paul had been caught with his hands down a pair of houndstooth pants. Paul had made a mistake messing with one of their own: the town fathers sent him packing. During another short stay I went back to the place where Paul had parked his Thunderbird and given me my first taste, near the old Woolgemuth farm. I even fixed heroin there, in the futile hope that whatever portal had been opened on that long-ago afternoon would be opened for me again.

At sixteen I found myself back in Vancouver, back on the Corner. Two years gone but I entered into the rhythm of the street so quickly you'd think I'd only been to the bathroom. I heard that Kitty had dropped some Purple Rain and gone to Haight Ashbury to find herself. I spent Christmas that year in the solitary cells under the old cow barns in Oakalla prison, for selling some bunk pot to an undercover agent.

Once I got out I went back east again, to London, where I took up with a hooker named Big Julie and acquired a methamphetamine habit. When shooting crystal got too weird, I found myself another nurse who cried over the tracks on my arms. When she ran out of tears, and went back to her life, I took my madness to Toronto. Wired to the yin-yang on a $500-a-day habit, I picked up a Saturday Night Special.

Before Christmas of 1970, I was charged with three bank robberies. The hold-up squad had beaten me so badly I had to be arraigned in early morning magistrate's court wearing a garbage bag over my head. Don Jail officials turned me away at the front gate — I was sent to St. Michael's Hospital instead, where my jaw was wired, my broken teeth pulled, my forehead sutured, and my ribs strapped back into place. After two weeks of being handcuffed to the hospital bed, I was returned to the Don and admitted. The doctor waiting to do my intake medical, in a joyless cinderblock room, was Paul. I had learned he'd recently received five years for sexual assault and administrating a narcotic to a minor, and gathered he was being made to serve his sentence as a somewhat glorified orderly. He sat behind a bare table, wearing an ugly white smock, and went down the perfunctory checklist, never raising his eyes from my file photograph, asking questions in a monotone. When we were done he didn't ask me if I was in any pain, and I didn't ask him for any morphine. A month shy of my twenty-first birthday, a judge handed me ten-years in Canada's oldest prison, Kingston Penitentiary.

My second night in the pen an old dope fiend named Suitcase Simpson hooked me up with a handful of pills. The head keeper saw me crossing the dome on the wobble and sway and ran me straight to the hole. He charged me for "condition other than normal," or C.O.N. for short. It was a charge I would receive frequently, and a condition I would aspire to for the next few years.

Prisons are about addictions. Most prisoners are casualties of their own habits. They have all created victims — some in cruel and callous ways — but almost to a man they have first practised that cruelty on themselves. Prison provides the loneliness that fuels addiction. It is the slaughterhouse for addicts, and all are eventually delivered to its gates.

When we were lucky and got a package in, we used homemade rigs — syringes made from ballpoint pens and coat hangers. Other times we cooked down Darvons and cough syrup from the infirmary, or stole yeast and tomato juice from the kitchen to make a brew. We did what we could to get past the four corners of our cells.

Eventually I was transferred to a medium-security facility. I decided to throw the dope to the ground and look for another kind of escape. Within eight months I had a hook 'n' ladder play happening and was living the life of a fugitive in Ottawa, where I met Paddy Mitchell and Lionel Wright; the three of us became known as the Stopwatch Gang. For the next dozen or so years, heroin ceased to be at the centre of my universe. I sipped whiskey to soothe the beast but I was too busy to chase a dope habit. We stole millions of dollars, racked up nine escapes between the three of us, and made the Most Wanted list in two countries. By Halloween of 1980 the FBI had caught up with me in Arizona. They dragged me off to the ultimate penitentiary, Marion, Illinois.

Four years later I was transferred to Canada. I had grown bone-weary of prison culture and my criminal lifestyle. I went to my cell one day, closed my door, and began to write. When my head came up a year later I had the first draft of a novel. I sent the manuscript to Fred Desroches, a criminologist at the University of Waterloo, who passed it on to their writer-in-residence, Susan Musgrave. Susan became my editor, then my wife, in a maximum-security wedding. I published *Jackrabbit Parole*, and a year later I was released.

We moved to Vancouver Island, to a vine-covered cottage by the sea. I bought a weedeater and a pink bicycle for my stepdaughter, Charlotte. I planted annuals. I began to engage with a new matrix of friends; I planted perennials. For the first two years I fixed up our home, pounding nails and painting trim. Susan and I had a second daughter, Sophie. I began another novel but found myself staring for hours at a blank page. I had been released from prison, but still I had not escaped. I felt the same aloneness in the midst of my warrant-burning party in our garden as I had in my grade nine class. Once again I went in search of the only solace I knew.

~·~·~

The only real serenity I have ever experienced in life, paradoxically and tellingly, has been without the assistance of drugs. It arose from a long period of abstinence, late in life, encouraged by the love of my wife and my daughters, nurtured by my friends, and witnessed by a God of my understanding — in whom, ultimately, I could not extinguish my addiction.

But even after a lifetime, I was not done with my crimes, nor were they done with me. In 1999 I returned to a full-blown heroin and cocaine habit. I had tried to keep a foot in each world, to hold onto the weight of love and family, but was pulled into the underworld of drugs. I chose to destroy both lives — not in a calculated way, more by default, but I chose nonetheless. I committed the worst bank robbery of my life, an unprofessional, unprovoked act of violence. It cost me an eighteen-year sentence, and nearly cost some people their lives.

Now, at fifty pieces, I find myself stripped bare, beaten back from hope, all out of illusions, in yet another prison cell. Having fallen through the crust of this earth so many times, it seems only on this small and familiar pad of concrete, where I can make seven steps in one direction, then take seven back, do my feet touch down with any certainty.

A year before my arrest, when Sophie was nine, we went out sliding after a freak snowfall. Hurtling down the hill on a red plastic saucer, we whirled faster and faster until the edge caught and we spilled. We tumbled through the snow, Sophie's pearly whites shining to the heavens, her laughter like small golden bells.

Now Sophie is twelve. When she accompanies her mother on their weekly visits to the prison, I hold her on my lap, and those wide brown eyes fix onto mine. Sophie needs to see me rise up again, return to her life. Though we are connected in unbreakable ways, I worry about her memories of a drug-addicted dad.

So I pace, seven steps one way, seven steps back. And I write. The days pass. I sit on my concrete pad, cross my legs and begin to breathe. The darkness of my world melts away, and as I move towards the mystery I can almost hear those faint golden bells. Slowly I enter the heart of unknowing, without expectation, without heroin.

LEAVING THEIR MARK

Leaving Their Mark

There is a scene in *Men in Prison* where Victor Serge stares at an ostensibly blank wall, which, upon closer inspection, reveals a labyrinth of scrawls, etched there by generations of prisoners.

Victor Serge's wall is in a French prison, more than half a century ago, but if you walked into the Victoria city lock-up today, where no writing instruments are permitted, the first thing to strike you would be the amount of writing scratched on the walls, into the tabletops, and scorched onto the ceilings.

There are odes to drugs, verses and curses, and scatological limericks aplenty. But, mostly there's just a name, a date, and sometimes the sad reason:

ANGEL — DEUCE LESS — B&E — APRIL/98 — FTW

So perfectly minimalist is this story that Raymond Carver himself could have adopted the form if he'd thought his readers might understand the language of jailhouse graffiti. The story tells us Angel is young because he's been sentenced to a reformatory term, and that he's a repeater, because the judge gave him the maximum two years less a day for break and enter. It's easy to imagine the rest, a young man lying on his bunk, freshly sentenced and awaiting transfer, trying to make sense of where he is, where he is going, and scratching words on the wall until it becomes real for him. Then, in an angry afterthought, adding the acronym. *Fuck the World.*

Like Angel, prisoners everywhere have felt the need to leave to leave their mark. In Kingston Penitentiary a novel was written in berry juice, in the Russian gulags journals were routinely inscribed on cigarette papers, and the poems of war prisoners have been found carved in bars of soap. Lady Jane Grey, awaiting execution in the Tower of London, supposedly pricked tiny holes in a piece of paper to form the words to a poem.

These voices come out of the dungeons and the labour camps and the penal colonies. This is writing from an experience, not about it.

CRIME AND PUNISHMENT (2000)

THE SORRY STATE OF PRISON LITERATURE in North America is almost criminal. There has been scarce good writing, let alone any great writing leaping over the walls.

In other times Solzhenitsyn was locked up by Stalin as Dostoevsky had been by the Czar; Hitler imprisoned Victor Frankel, amongst others. A communist regime placed Václav Havel in a cell and, on another continent, military juntas jailed and tortured Jacobo Timmerman.

What's wrong with this country? We fill our jails with junkies but have yet to produce one Genet. Maybe it's time for a good old-fashioned purge of the intellectual class: the political climate seems to be ripening. Put a few writers down for a hard time. How would a sequel to *Alias Grace* read after Peggy did a stint in the Kingston Pen? Deprive Mordecai of his Bordeaux and bottle him up in the real Bordeaux, a two-acre jail in Quebec where the Anglais are literally an endangered species. Or handcuff John Ralston Saul and lead him away . . . no, no, the image of Her Excellency wrestling to open a can of Five Alive on visiting day is too painful to bear.

If we don't want to lock up intellectuals maybe we could slam down a few journalists instead. To what end I'm not sure. Christie Blatchford would probably spend more time in the weight pit than at her computer and get yet more tattoos. June Callwood would organize all the women into a sit-down. Jan Wong would have problems holding her pen and a spoon, never mind hearing over the clatter of steel trays in the chow hall. David Frum would quickly become the warden's clerk and write glowing columns on the humane treatment of Canadian convicts, and why no other prisoner deserves what he, the David, is receiving.

Perhaps the days of prison literature have passed. Our society doesn't lock up intellectuals, and our culture doesn't encourage those locked up as criminals to learn to engage with their experience on any intellectual level. The discourse on crime and punishment, in our parliaments and newspapers, has been reduced to bumper stickers. *Zero Tolerance: Three Strikes and You're Out.* We are a society impatient with its misfits.

This procession towards orderly thought demands a moral consolation, not a confrontation. There is a turning away from the darkness and the turmoil, the wickedness and the sick livers. These things belong to someone else, something foreign, not us. No one wants these problems in their living room or in their literature.

There is no "noir" left in American crime novels; the characters are all Republicans. The best prison books are written by non-prisoners. A novel called *Green River Rising* occupies the American paradigm so perfectly, it is shocking to learn it was written by an albino psychologist (Tim Willocks) from London, England. No other recent fiction, with the exception of Edward Bunker's *The Hate Factory*, *Little Boy Blue* and *No Beast So Fierce*, comes close.

In the Belly of the Beast, a work of non-fiction by Jack Abbott, a prisoner, has a great title and comes from a hard-forged mind, but it is his literary mentor Norman Mailer who succeeded in a true crime book of his own, *The Executioner's Song*. The last major book to emerge from the dungeons in Canada was Roger Caron's

Go Boy, but this was more of a personal accomplishment than a blast from the zeitgeist.

The decline in the genre is inevitable in the context of the reigning critical correctness. The prison writings that are competent enough to be published today are either so filled with facile remorse as to be obvious, or so seduced by the requirements of entertainment they become tales of false bravado.

Rebuked by the public, prison authors have learned to write with shame, but not about it. Many choose to invert shame; most drown in it. The dignity so essential to authentic literature is not easily recovered in the aftermath of a crime and its punishment. The moral authority to express suffering is forfeited and everyone, reader and writer, in this age of absolutes feels uncomfortable stepping into the territory, the eventuality of reclamation. To enter through the gates of a prison, carrying the weight of your crimes, to hear that six-hundred pounds of steel slam shut, is to know absolute loss. Later we become belligerent or accepting, reflective or numb — often all of the above. But misfortune earned can become a profound privilege. To know absolute loss, to suffer real guilt, to look back on how you have betrayed most of what you thought of as decent and good — that is a stripped-down place indeed: a naked page on which to write down the lost language, that language which reflects the enormity of being born.

Prison writing, to survive, must return to that reflecting skin.

The Clockwork Grey of the CSC

THIRTY YEARS AGO, IN SIMPLER TIMES, I was sent to the penitentiary. They gave me a haircut, stitched a number above my breast pocket, and tossed me in a cell on the fish range. My biggest worry, besides my sentence, was whether I'd ever get the right-sized boots.

It's year 2000, and I'm back in prison. No haircut, I have to memorize my number, and my biggest worry is whether I'll get the right crimogenic index rating.

The fish range is now called an Assessment Centre. They have painted murals on the concrete, renamed guards correctional officers, prisoners have become inmates or even residents, we wear street clothes instead of blues, and there are more behaviour modification programs in here than bars.

The key to understanding the new paradigm in our prisons may lie in the corporate logo: the CSC. Corrections Services Canada — it works both forwards and backwards, and in both official languages. Thirty years ago this system was called the Canadian Penitentiary Services, and it wasn't forward looking, or working in anyone's language, so a handful of determined federal bureaucrats began to study some of the European models. They adapted them so well that Canada has become a world leader in penology. Other countries now come here to study us, even, belatedly, some Americans. America has gone through a twenty-five year devolution and their prisons are experiencing an unprecedented level of inhumanity and brutality. The Clockwork Grey of the new CSC seems a small price to pay to preserve our country's humanity. That said, this is an evolution with an absurd edge.

Designing programs and implementing them are the two solitudes of CSC. To order someone into therapy is often to subvert the purpose. Willingness is the key to change — you have to want it to get it. So there exists a jumping-through-hoops mentality by inmates, and an air of resignation on the part of the staff. But in fairness, the percentage of inmates who genuinely wish to change, and the calibre of instructors willing to help them is much higher than the skeptics would have us believe.

My Regional Reception Assessment Centre Handbook informs me I'll be here for ten to fourteen weeks, during which time I'll be evaluated, assessed, analyzed, tested, probed and profiled. A team of IPOs, CO2s, psychologists and unit managers will collect, collate, graph and interpret the data. They will determine risk factors, crime cycles, pen placement, treatment programs and how much fibre I'll need in my diet. It could be argued, and convincingly, that this is the evolution of penology.

The handbook is a humourless text, but as I read the earnest descriptions of available programs I can't help but wonder/speculate. The Violent Offender Program? Would Billy the Kid have emerged nine months later as Billy the Inner Child? Anger Management? Could Vinnie Mad Dog Coll have become, Assertive Dog Coll? Would Bonnie and Clyde, made to enrol in Skills for a Healthy Relationship, have come to terms with their co-dependency and been granted a conjugal visit? Pushed into taking Cognitive Skills, Machine Gun Kelly would soon identify his trigger thoughts. Ma Barker, in her seventh week of Family

Violence Circle might have reached the stunning conclusion she'd been a life-long enabler.

I'm ahead of myself. Before anyone reaches their inner child or enabling self, they have to take tests. Lots of tests. It is tests that drive the modern personal correctional plan.

My favourite so far has been the 560-odd questionnaire called the Minnesota Multi-Phasic Personality Index. Never mind that it has been proved culturally biased and hopelessly flawed, the centrefold of my "critical needs assessment" will be determined by questions like, "Have you ever wanted to be a girl?" Think of the possibilities. Had the question been, "Have you ever wanted to be a woman?" I might have answered differently. But a girl? Did they mean a child, or a grrrl, or is "girl" what they still call a woman in Minnesota? Think, think. If I were a grrrl I could have a conjugal visit with myself. No, better play it safe and mark False.

Next question, "Do you love your mother? Or, if she's dead, did you?" You don't stop loving someone just because they're dead, but my mother is alive and I love her very much so I mark True.

"Do you believe you are being controlled by an unseen force?" Like an unavailable Warden? Or does this mean subliminal advertising and the all-pervasive consumer culture? I glance at the woman administering the test — she is staring back with the look of someone who thinks more along the lines of, "Did Satan order you to rob that bank?" I circle False.

I'm most intrigued with, "If you were a reporter, would you like to report on the theatre?" At first, this seems McCarthyesque, as in would you like to keep an eye on those socialist homosexual so-called actors? Of course it could also mean if you were a reporter wouldn't you prefer to report on child poverty or political corruption? In other words, something substantial. But, I like the theatre! Besides, if it's good theatre it deals with child poverty and political corruption. Stop thinking, just answer the question.

Okay, True. I'll be a pansy art critic. At least I didn't say I wanted to be a girl, even if I did.

"Would you like to be a florist?" No, no. no. Read my lips. Give me some questions on hockey here, or how about them Blue Jays, eh?

I handed in my test, unfinished. I figured if I didn't have a personality they would assign me one.

Next came the real pick of the litter, the Psychopathy Check List Revised. It determines, unequivocally, whether you're a psychopath or not. I remembered John Gray, our John Gray, the playwright, not the Venus and Mars guy, interviewing the author of this test. John used the doctor's own statistics to extrapolate the fact that there had to be, at minimum, 40,000 psychopaths living in British Columbia. With a couple of hundred locked away in prisons that still left 39,800 odd psychos at large. The good doctor reassured John these were people who put their psychopathy to good use. They lived productive, well-adjusted lives as surgeons, CEOs and ambulance drivers.

The light bulb went on. The CSC doesn't have to go through all these gyrations to reprogram anyone, they just have to find every inmate the right job!

Psychos become CEOs. Bookmakers could work for the 6/49 Lotto Corporation. The government weenies currently running Sports Action Lotteries are rank amateurs compared to real bookmakers. The action would double in three months. Small time drug dealers could be issued white smocks and put behind the pharmacy counter. Dispensing fees are ten times the markup on an eightball of cocaine. A B&E artist would slip like a crowbar into the home security business. In custom protecting your home he could charge you more for alarm systems than what he could steal from your house, anyway.

The weight pit crews, all pumped up and tattooed down, could be recruited for the WWF Raw. They would take wrestling to new levels and earn up to ten thousand a night, just for being themselves. Even those criminals too corrupt or too incorrigible to be anything else, could hang out a shingle and practise law. The worst that could happen is nobody would notice.

But the CSC is not an employment agency. Its self-determined mandate is to reconcile the twin towers of punishment and rehabilitation, a difficult enough task without the public, political and media scorn. It takes a certain brand of courage — some would call foolhardy, some would call moral — to continue to pursue a humanitarian vision of Corrections, but to abandon course now would surely be a "Mistake".

In simpler times, on that fish range thirty years ago, I was celled with a young man, one of the last to get the paddle. One of his memories, besides the scars on his skin, was of being bound at the ankles and wrists and having a hood pulled over his head. He was the last of a dozen men that day, and he remembers the hood, the inside being cold and slick with the mucous and spittle and blood from the broken lips of those who went before him.

I've spent years in American prisons, and more years inside here in Canada. I've observed the public mood in this country. I know the CSC vision is all that stands between me and a black hood filled with the blood and the fear of my fellow prisoners.

The Zen of the Chain

It's five in the morning and the deuces squad is standing six strong in front of your cell. The Lieutenant drops about forty pounds of chains on the cement floor and beckons you forward. You rub the sleep out of your eyes; you are confused. You haven't applied for a transfer and for damned sure it's not an early release. You have no idea what these guys got in mind but you know it can't be good.

Get steady boyo because whatever it is you've done to piss them off, the Bureau of Prisons has decided to disappear you, put you on the ghost chain. You are about to enter into the perpetual transfer zone. Every morning you will be wrapped up in waist chains and leg manacles, tossed aboard a bus or a plane and shipped around the country doing one night stands in prison isolation wings from California to Georgia and from Minnesota to Texas — for as long as the Bureau deems necessary. Welcome to the nightmare world of Diesel Therapy.

Twelve Step Survival Guide for the Transfer Tour:

1. Don't protest; it only makes them feel better. Don't ask where you are going, or why, they will only lie to you anyway. And don't ask to take anything, even a toothbrush. You can't.

2. When you kneel on the bench for them to put the leg shackles on, point your toes as far back as you can. Stretching the tendon on the front of the ankle will provide just that squidge of space between you and the steel bracelet when you return to a standing position. Your ankle bones will be grateful at the end of each day.

3. Start to grow your thumbnails.

4. On the first bus away from your home prison there will be faces you know from the compound, maybe even a friend. They will all be speculating on where you're headed and why. Listen to none of it. They don't know a godamned thing. Their jaws are working from the same nervous energy you're feeling. As you get deeper into the trip these familiars will be dropped off or sent off in different directions and soon you are doing the daylight bus rides with strangers. You will feel completely alone, because you are. Within a week you will forget you ever had friends.

5. You will notice that the seating arrangements on both the buses and the planes are colour coded. No matter how enlightened you believe you are on the issue of race, obey the colour code. If you're white, sit in the white section, if black be on black. America's prisons are the front lines of an undeclared race war. Don't be naive about it. Otherwise, one night your cellie is going to be a bald-headed bigot, who upon removing his shirt reveals two lightning bolts rippling across his chest and his enquiring mind wants to know "why you been woofing it up with the niggers all day?" Or if black, "why you been sitting side that blue-eyed devil all trip?" Either way it isn't a question you want to have to answer while locked up in a tight space.

6. A small white box will be tossed into your lap each day. This is lunch. It is, and it always will be, a pimento loaf sandwich on white bread and one of those pale oranges with the thin skin that

is so hard to peel — even without handcuffs. This is why you are growing your thumbnails.

7. At each stop you will always be put in the transfer unit and unless you are the caliber of Pablo Escobar or have the heat of Timothy fuckin' McVeigh, you will be double bunked. So to avoid the monster racist or the rabid homo rapist, spend at least part of each day selecting your cellie for that night. It won't always work, but after you've been processed through induction at the prison du jour, make an agreement with, and stay in close proximity to, the person of your choice. The Looey doing cell assignments just wants a quick, no fuss lockup and no overnight incidents to have to write up so he will usually go along with your play.

8. If they haven't issued it already ask for toilet paper, towels, and soap. It's usually in a cleaner's closet at the front of the tier as you come in. Once the door slams on your drum that's it. You ain't getting out for nothing and there ain't no tier tender to go fetch you something either. The next time you see anybody it'll be five AM and he'll be pushing cornflakes and blue milk in a cardboard bowl through your food slot.

9. Always treasure hunt. Check the bullpen and later your assigned cell for contraband. Feel under the benches, along any ledges, inside toilet bowls. Investigate the lump in your mattress. You never know when you'll get lucky, when someone's had to dump something or simply forgot. A handcuff key, a paper of dope, whatever.

10. You will have minimal contact with a few of the static prisoners from each joint — the one who brings your morning cornflakes or the guy who takes your picture during induction. Don't bother trying to get a message to your mother or your girl or your lawyer out through these guys. They have been handpicked; they are near you for a reason.

11. Two types to avoid on the chain at all costs:

(A) The Jailhouse Lawyer. A guy who uses words like mandamus and habeas corpus and who complains to the marshals non-stop how all this is all an abuse of his human rights and against the laws of America.

(B) The Stone Cold Desperado. The guy hobbling across the tarmac flanked on all sides by about fifteen escorts and he has a marshal bringing up the rear holding a ten-foot trip chain attached to his leg manacles. You can bet your pimento sandwich that this guy is just off a fresh homicide, with zero to lose. In all likelihood he has a sharpened toothbrush hidden up his ass and he's just looking for a warm body to stab up.

Do not sit near either of these guys even if it means violating the colour code. Because every marshal on the plane owns his personal copy of the *Con Air* video and he's waiting to even the score. These badged-up, uniform-wearing mothers load their Remingtons and strap on their Glocks every morning the way the rest of us brush our teeth and pull on our socks. You give off even a hint of trouble and the marshals will not only violate your civil rights, they will ventilate them. Just be aware of who you're riding next to because when they use a shotgun you've only got to be in the vicinity.

12. Somehow the homos and the snitches and the strip searches and the marshals and the killers and the five AM roll-ups after cornflakes in blue milk seem to all get jumbled together in the endless miles of bad road you've been travelling for too long. To survive you must find the zen of the chain. For instance, if you're unfortunate enough to have a black box designation and you have to wear that uncomfortable contraption over your handcuffs all day, don't dwell on the cramps and pain it causes, flow with it, become your black box. Don't be a new wave crack baby criminal, don't go sissy on yourself. Suck up them fumes, concentrate on your breathing, find your mantra. Diesel in, diesel out. Let that

which doesn't kill you make you stranger. Transform yourself and your busload of fellow maniacs into an edgy version of Ken Kesey and his band of merry pranksters. Be patient in all things, let the seasons come and go, and one day fortune will smile. The bus will rumble to a stop at some front gate and you will walk in, passing by enough piles of coiled razor wire to make a knife, fork, and spoon for every man, woman, and child on the subcontinent of India. You will step into the induction area, they'll take off the chains and do the strip fan. You'll get dressed again but this time the bulls will direct you to the right. And just like that you're walking down a corridor towards a mainline. You feel weightless. You have survived. Life is grand. Until next time.

Hooked

Two judges, in less than one year and on separate occasions, have sentenced me to life, and to death — of sorts. The first one took away my freedom and the second one didn't take away my cigarettes.

The first judge gave me an eighteen-year prison sentence, which in terms of parole eligibility is the same as a life sentence for murder. But it was the second judge, Justice Sunni Stromberg-Stein, who did the real damage. She overturned a WCB/Solicitor General conspiracy to ban all smoking in BC jails. Now that I can smoke cigarettes as fast as I can roll them I don't know if I'll live long enough to finish this bit. Doing time is easy, quitting cigarettes is hard. I've got long history at both.

I've quit before. Once for seven years, another for four, and a thousand times for an hour or two. And I'm in Carl Sagan numbers for the times I've intended to, or promised someone I would — soon. Starting tomorrow.

I started smoking young but didn't catch a serious habit until I turned eleven. My first brand was Craven A, mostly because Old Man Hallett kept them on the shelf in his drugstore right opposite where he was distracted by people buying bus tickets out of the small northern Ontario town I was growing up in. That same year I was introduced to morphine. The doctor who unzipped my childhood would afterwards deliver a lecture on the hazards of smoking.

By the time I became old enough to buy my own bus ticket out of town, I had changed brands. On the streets of Vancouver, at the age of thirteen, I learned how to buy my own drugs and my own cigarettes. It was never a love story.

Seventeen years later I was living in Arizona, a Marlboro man under an American alias, on the run in two countries from six different police forces. I had managed to escape prison three times, was living drug clean, but had never got free from the cigarettes. I was always looking for the easy, the painless, the instant, the guaranteed way out. Then I saw the ad for the money-back guaranteed Shick Stop Smoking Program.

Americans know how to sell health, or anything else: imbue it with sexiness. I flew down to Phoenix, parked my Mooney 201, rented a car, and scooted up to the glass and steel Shick office tower, all ficas and ferns, and polished faux marble foyer. The personable blonde receptionist confirmed my appointment and took down a little personal history (all lies, since I was a fugitive) and buzzed me through another set of doors to meet my counsellor, another attractive human being, a little smoother. She took down some more of my lies, then told me she expected me to commit to four sessions on four consecutive days, and that I had to cough up nine hundred charlies, plus tax, on the spot. How could I refuse? I'd already been there ten minutes, in the company of two different and beautiful women: to bail out now would be like welching. So I reached into the sky rocket and anted up a stack of twenties. More accustomed to a cheque or plastic, her smile changed only slightly and for a brief moment, then she counted the twenties back like a banker and slid them into a drawer.

I signed the contract — we were to begin in a few days — and shook her hand goodbye. I stopped to pick up a couple of cartons of Marlboros on my way back to the airport. My counsellor said I had to bring cigarettes to my first appointment.

I flew home, drove back up to my house in the canyon, confident that I would soon be puffing my last. The next morning the FBI kicked the doors in.

I spent a couple of nights in the Flagstaff jail, then I was transferred down to the Maricopa County lockup in downtown Phoenix. They ran me up four breathless flights of stairs to the super-max wing — a dingy row of cells — and locked me down. I was dying for a smoke so I called out to the Mexican in the cell beside me. The next thing I saw were his fat brown fingers holding out a shag rolly. I took this misshapen excuse for a cigarette, loose shreds of tobacco spilling out both ends, and was about to ask for a light when it dawned on me: this was the day I was supposed to be sitting opposite my beautiful personal counsellor in the upscale office across town. I started to think about the nine hundred American, plus tax, and tossed the shag in the toilet, pushed the button, and never smoked again, until . . .

Four years later when I was sitting on the segregation unit in Marion, Illinois. There had been a riot in the chow hall at the evening meal. I wasn't involved but had been standing too close to a guy who got his throat cut and spewed blood all over my pants; they scooped me up in the aftermath. My friend Alan, who was involved, was locked up next to me; when his door opened for a shower, he stopped in front of my cell and put two Camels and a match on my food slot. "Alan," I said, "you know I don't smoke; them things are bad for you." Alan laughed, "Look at you. Sitting buck naked on the floor of the Chinese cell in the worst joint in the whole federal system. How much worse can it get? Here, fire one of these up, maybe you'll get lucky and get cancer."

Two weeks later the warden found me not guilty in the chow hall massacre, and released me back to the mainline. On my way back to my unit I stopped by the commissary and picked up two cartons of Camels.

You've never been hooked until you've been hooked on Camels. Another year passed: first thing each morning I tapped out one of those non-filter Turkish blend little suckers and fired it up. The smoke hit bottom like an overhead right to the lungs. I was wired to the hilt by the time they sent me home to a Canadian prison, where it was nothing but Export A and Drum tobacco. I threw cigarettes to the ground again.

Not a few years later the clock ran out on my sentence and I was released. I went to work pounding nails for a skinny carpenter who smoked the longest, strongest cigarettes you can buy and still be called a Canadian. This guy went all day, a cigarette dangling out the corner of his mouth, driving six-inch spikes in three clean swings. I figured it must be in the cigarettes; by the time I got the hang of pounding spikes and learned it had nothing to do with cigarettes, I was hooked again. I finally got lucky with a film script, and was able to quit the heavy labour, but by then I was pounding back a pack a day of Players Light.

Meanwhile my youngest daughter developed a habit of her own: breaking my cigarettes, lecturing me on second-hand smoke, leaving pictures of black and tarry lungs on my pillow, and telling me how my clothes smelled bad. How I stank. I caved in and quit again.

A couple of years after that my daughter and I took a five-star holiday to Cuba. While my eight-year-old danced the Macarena with the hotel dance instructor, I started up a conversation with an elderly Cuban gentleman who rolled Cohiba Robustos in the lobby. What could be the harm in an occasional fine cigar? Even my daughter agreed: cigars are cool. I returned home with five boxes in my suitcase.

By the second box I was inhaling, and I'd stopped handing them out. When my stock ran out I went to the local tobacconist to replenish it. A box of the cigars I bought in Cuba, I discovered, cost, in Canada, about the same as a used BMW. Before long I was smoking smaller and smaller cigars until I was right back down to cigarettes.

Now both my daughters were on my case. The older one had turned fifteen and was far too mature to smoke. She'd quit, and she was riding me the way only a reformed fifteen-year-old smoker can. Time to get quit again.

The patch. Great dreams but it made my skin itchy, and I got so-so results. I asked my doctor to prescribe Zyban: Zyban appealed to me because you got to keep smoking for the first part of the regime. But I wasn't only taking the Zyban, I was eating Percodans all day. One Zyban, ten Percodans. It didn't seem to be having the desired effect. The way cigars led me back to cigarettes, the Percodans took me back to heroin, which in turn put me back on the wrong side of a prison wall.

As I awaited trial, and the announcement of Sheldon Green's (BC Attorney General's office) and the WCB-ordained smoking ban in BC jails, I continued to light up. A few days before New Year's, no smoking ban in sight yet, they tossed me in the hole — for possession of a contraband X-Acto knife blade. I was going to use it to slit my throat if I couldn't quit. Prohibited from smoking, I managed to quit for two days, then a few minutes before midnight the youngster in the adjacent cell fished me over a contraband cigarette. It was the eve of the new millennium: that was my last cigarette. Of the 20th century, that is.

Now that I've been transferred to the federal system maybe there is something I can do to spite both judges. Quit, just because one said I didn't have to, and by doing that maybe win back the years the other one sentenced me to.

A WCB spokesperson characterized Justice Sunni Stromberg-Stein's ban on the smoking ban as "a bump in the road." For most cigarette addicts it's been a long road, a road as straight and flat as a run of bad luck.

THE CARVING SHED

A CURTAIN OF RAIN FALLS SOFTLY across the tin roof, mixing like a snare drum with the rhythm of Frog Lake on the tape player. There is the smell of red cedar and the shadows of two men carving in silent concentration. The shed is Native Brotherhood territory but I'm welcomed here not just because my great-grandmother was Ojibway, but because in the eyes of the Brotherhood, anyone who has done as many years in a white man's prison as I have must be all right.

Under the yellow light tacked to the crossbeam, our little carving shed becomes a world unto itself. Space and time seem to pause together and suspend the three of us in a gift of place. The razor wire, the gun towers, the years behind us, and the years ahead don't hold much weight in the curve of this moment.

Bobby kicks the cedar shavings from a moon mask he's been working on into a small pile. Narcisse, an elder, who has been whittling a talking stick, unfolds his tobacco pouch and rolls a cigarette. No hurry, we're on Indian time as he's fond of saying. I mark my page in a new hardcover I'm reading, Eden Robinson's *Monkey Beach*, the story of young Haisla "Flower", a girl coming of age in the coastal village of Kitamat.

I turn Bobby's moon mask in my hands, checking the depths of the cuts, running my thumbs along the swirling grain. I pass the mask to Narcisse. Bobby is encouraged enough by Narcisse's silent inspection to suggest mother of pearl for the eyes. Narcisse says "abalone shell."

Young Shawn comes running in out of the rain. He squeezes the water from his ponytail, his long blue-black hair as shiny as a crow's tail, hangs his soaked benny on a nail. Underneath he's wearing a sweat top illustrated with a pair of manacled hands and the words "Free Leonard Peltier". Shawn made the sweater's logo when he first drove up on this bit but in the ensuing months his consciousness has shifted from the political towards the spiritual and his red fist has become unclenched. He says now of the sweater, "It's more like wearing a poppy, to remember, plus it keeps me warm."

Shawn reaches under the workbench and makes me a present of one of his drums, a caribou hide stretched over a pine frame. Last week, I helped him bang out a gradual release plan and filled in the corresponding applications. Afterwards we sat together to write a different letter, this one to his *Tsinii* Al up in Haida Gwaii. I had to dig it out of him to find words, his words, to make it his voice and his letter. Shawn had come down from Masset and landed in the East End of Vancouver. When the pavement came between him and the earth, he fell into confusion, addiction, and when welfare was no longer enough, he became involved in senseless crime. Many of his friends ended up in small boxes in cheap funeral homes but Shawn ended up here in a bigger box. Prison, is, simply put, the bottom rung of the welfare ladder.

The Correctional Service of Canada tries. They recognize the gulf between native and white rehabilitation. They encourage the Native Brotherhood to function, they hire native contract workers to act as counsellors, teachers and Elders. They allow the carving shed, the sweat lodge, and a private space for healing circles. In spite of the tension and mistrust from both sides, the red path is attainable — if a native prisoner recovers his culture, he recovers himself.

Tonight, Shawn's face is etched in troubled lines as deep as Bobby's mask. He tells me he wanted to take the money from selling his drums and make restitution to his ex-landlady, the woman who returned home to broken locks, smashed lamps, and missing valuables. Case management had turned him down, stating there is no process within Corrections to make restitution without a court order.

A hundred years ago, Shawn would have faced his victim and his village in a longhouse. Restitution would have been part of the determination. Shawn would have been punished and the circle would have been damaged but it would not have been broken.

In Eden Robinson's story, her uncle Mickey has just landed on the doorstep after a long absence. He's been "away." Uncle Mickey is wearing a "Free Leonard Peltier" T-shirt. But as Uncle Mickey begins an overnight boat trip, taking young Lisa Marie up to the traditional oolichan fishing grounds, I suspect that out there amongst the seals and Kermode bears, where the dark water laps at the stone beaches and bleached logs stick out like old bones, that Uncle Mickey will not be denied his process, the one that existed there ten thousand years before the first iron bar was ever poured.

In the Company of Women

Usually a bobby pin lying in a puddle on concrete wouldn't make me stop and stare in wonder, but there I was, dead in my tracks. Maybe it was because the puddle was on the caged-in roof yard of a maximum security segregation unit in Matsqui, a men's prison.

Maybe it was because last week I went to bed with seven women. Of the seven, I had met five previously at various social functions. One of them I married. Each of them lies between the covers of a tantalizing little book titled, *Desire, In Seven Voices*, a collection of essays edited by Lorna Crozier.

Although the introduction alludes to all sorts of mystical connections to the number seven, I have put my own spin on it. I have been using the book the way a convict puts an X on the wall, an essay to mark each passing day. A week of women.

Monday, I was in a cool blue room with Evelyn Lau; Tuesday I blushed with Bonnie Burnard as she wrote about the hard evidence of desire. On Wednesday, I fell in love with Shani Mootoo's tender admissions. Thursday, I had dinner and went to Paris with Carol Shields. On Friday, I wanted to eat the snow off of Lorna Crozier's mittens. It's Saturday and I'm driving with my wife, Susan

Musgrave. She's got the top down and she's over the speed limit. I wanted to smoke a cigarette afterwards. A Number 7 of course.

As I bent to pick up the bobby pin, I remembered I was being closely observed by three young women in uniform on the other side of the smoked-glass office windows. The bobby pin was my *red wheelbarrow/glazed with rainwater/beside the white chickens* moment.

Most of my free life has been spent in the company of women and their objects. I grew up with five sisters and the quintessential mother. I'm married with two daughters, and our house is usually filled with their girlfriends, most whom treat me as their confidante or other dad. Even four of our five cats are females. But I'm still trying to get used to being guarded by women.

One of them comes to open the grill with a key the size of a garden trowel. My yard time is up. She is polite, so am I. We have formed the relationship. I'm an old con, in every sense of the word; a deferential drop of the eyes gets me through all the gates in any prison, except the front one.

I have a relationship with all three of these guards. They are the day shift, in charge of the fifteen or so segregation prisoners. I am not in seg per se, I work up here. I serve the meals, I wash, fold, and issue the laundry, and I mop the floors the women walk on. I've come a long way, baby.

Female guards are the most professional within the Corrections community. They must not only be guards, they have to be guarded. When one of them summons me for a chore or a lockdown, she addresses me by last name only. I know their names by the tag pinned to their blouses but I avoid using them.

When they give me a pat-down search, I blush. There is nothing sexual, nothing intimate, about their hands on my body. I blush because this touching makes us all less human.

These three young women in another setting, would be friends of my daughter, or neighbours I would wave to as they passed by on their bicycles, or even students in my writing workshops. Sometimes a bobby pin in a puddle on concrete is the saddest object.

I like solitary, but I like this better, working up here. I have the relative quietude, but also a bit of freedom. And I've got a cleaner's closet to which I can retreat. I keep a chair in the narrow space between the washers and the dryers on one side, and the shelves filled with puffed wheat, tins of brown sugar, and boxes of styrofoam cups on the other. It's there, in my little cubbyhole, between the smell of warm towels and toasted cereals, where I read and try not to think.

A critic once described me as someone who thinks things. It became a household joke. Whenever I would be staring off into space as if the grief of the world were on my shoulders, and a visitor would ask "What's the matter with him?" my wife would answer, "Oh, that's just Stephen, he thinks things." But my best thinking got me into this cubbyhole: I pick up my book and turn to the page I left off at.

I love writers for what they do. These women's essays touch me in the most intimate ways of all, yet the words jump over gender and make me, for the reading, a little more human.

The buzzer on the dryer sounds. Another cycle done, time to fold towels. Tomorrow will bring Sunday *but* who can predict where Dionne Brand will take desire.

I tuck the little book in amongst the pile of towels just as a key raps loudly on the door, followed by a female voice. *Reid! Food carts up.* It was her way of letting me know it is time to serve meals.

Come Monday, with *Desire* depleted, I'll have to find a new book. Maybe there's one out there titled *Amnesia, in 6,570 Voices*, one to forget each passing day.

Bushwhacking South of the Border

THE LAST TIME I READ A *PLAYBOY* MAGAZINE, Jimmy Carter (who, by the way, would have known how to properly treat Saddam — he would have built him a new house) was the President of the United States. But hey, fuck the war and fuck the decline of the American presidency; what is of real significance here is the demise of pubic hair on American women. I had my first gape score at a centrefold in a lot of years and whoa and behold! Miss April got no hair down there!

I flipped to the other pictorials only to discover they all wore the same prepubescent vertical smile. I know these models have to be at least twenty-one to win a staple through their nipple from Hef, so how come most sport none, or very little, pubic hair? Even those who retain a thin wispy line have a *mons veneris* that looks more like a "Got Milk" commercial than the garden patch of a grown woman.

I have been in prison for too long, haven't viewed erotica for even longer. I sense that something of great social and cultural import has passed me by. Where did all those dark and curly Bermuda triangles disappear to? And when? It's like I fell asleep one night, and, in a reverse Rip Van Winkle, the whole continent got busy with the shaving cream. But an even more meaty question stared out at me from between the legs of this new fashion mode. Why?

Why, since I last looked, have pubic hairs, at least the public pubes, been clipped, cut, tonsured, trimmed, shaved, depilatoried, mowed, and mohawked? Perhaps G-string thongs and ittier-bittier bikini bottoms have moved women to narrow even further that thin middle line of modesty. But bikinis of all sizes have been around since Frankie danced with Annette and only a slight cropping was all that's ever been needed to make a wedge suitable for the viewing audience. And when it comes down to the G-string, modesty is no longer even in the movie. So why have all the nether goatees been so ruthlessly and utterly hacked into nothingness?

It is only the nothingness that is new to me. Women I've known have always had a penchant for pruning. I once had a girlfriend who shaped hers into a heart for Valentine's. I knew another who clipped her fiancée's into a diamond on their engagement night, and then there was an all-girls band in the '70s who contoured theirs into little guitars. But this modern vogue, this movement toward clear cutting, is a whole other slice of the honey pie.

Young women who like a clean line must, at least in part, inherit their crisp aesthetics from computer era imagery. Sort of a Laura Croft imitation. Or maybe it's global warming. There are evolutionary raisons d'etre for body hair and one of them is warmth. Perhaps with the earth temperature rising there is just too much heat down there in the pearly kitchen. How then do we explain the bare labes of those northern girls, especially the ones living above the 49th parallel? Do their lips stick to the crossbar in sub-zero weather? Surely in a country where the national symbol is the beaver, the pelt is not going to become extinct?

In another evolutionary trick, hair south of the navel is there to trap pheromones in its tangled locks. Pheromones are those little dancing musk devils produced to attract the opposite sex — in the case of the female body, to lure the unsuspecting male of the species towards her cave. Perhaps women who shave are making a statement. They choose not to trap men with a beguiling scent, opting for a more open, more conscious and less subliminal means of attraction. If true, some would have to ask themselves hard questions about perfume.

Pubic hair also acts as the local police force: it's there to serve and protect, to prevent friction and act as a buffer. But with the advent of the female jock strap, hair does present a feeble sort of protection. Some women may see it as simply obsolete.

Whatever all the different reasons women are trimming, there is one I know to be true. It is because their sexual partners prefer them that way. This is some cultural/generational preference I am not getting. Maybe my generation just didn't convey our wishes.

Something else changed with the young and the restless. I didn't grow up with Sex Ed classes being about AIDS and hepatitis and all the STDs. I didn't learn in grade six that condoms were as necessary as looking both ways before you cross the street. What is there to say to a generation of young lovers that has been taught sex is death, that there is a deadly virus lurking behind every bush? Small wonder they are not looking for a mystery lair. They don't want to peer through the undergrowth, nor their garden to be secret. They want a visible and clear shot at whatever they are getting into. Maybe it is the search for prepubescence itself because, at an even more subtle level, theirs is a generation that loses its innocence at a way too tender age.

After my initial shock and bewilderment at seeing Miss April with the southern isosceles of a ten-year-old, things have gone from bad to worse. I have since learned, while out in the compound talking about this phenomenon to a new generation of cons, that it is now common for young men to shave — and I'm not talking five o'clock shadows here. It's some sort of buff image trip. I been in the weight pit off and on for over a century, and I believe if you aren't bulked like Arnie or at least be flexing muscles in the professional ring then you got to be like fireman calendar gay to be waxing the hair off your body.

The boys in the gym have tried to convince me that clean shaven bodies are more attractive to the opposite sex, but I'm not even going there. Overly hirsute men are a turn-off for most of the women I've talked with, though I have heard of those with fetishes for thick back hair (they call these men "Bears"). Knowing that didn't make me want to jump into a barrel of Rogaine and neither will I now go soak in a vat of depilatory cream, even though I believe this new body gloss is much more than a fetish or a passing craze.

The trend is hooked to something deeper, caught up in a culture that has been relentlessly exposed to the concept marketing of an ideal human body. We have been sold on buns of steel, six-pack abs, cosmetic implants, and total makeovers ad infinitum. The perfection of body image seems within our grasp and we have come to see the ideal as more real than our own.

In the age of sophisticated software, a perfect design can be achieved with the simple click of a mouse. But is it real? Or is it the same virtual perfection we are trying to click on to in our lives? What makes us human, what keeps our worlds real? It can be found in the imperfection of our bodies, in the imperfect way they move through this world.

Our bodies are made to be lived in, so celebrate your nicks and scars, adorn the skin with tattoos if you like, manicure your pubes to your heart's content but always remember the rounded tummy or the small droop in the imperfect breast is the one with soul. If I were you, my little playboys and dixie chicks, I would guard my imagination — and most of my pubic hairs — against the onslaught of virtual beauty, because when the party is over and the morning light finds you alone in a spinning bed, afraid you might be flung off the edges of the earth, a thick swatch of hair might be all you have to hang on to.

THERE ARE NO CHILDREN'S BOOKS IN PRISON

AT 9:45 EVERY MORNING THE MAIN DOORS to A27 open and a crowd emerges. Most of the men are already rolling cigarettes from their green MacDonald tobacco pouches, not wanting to miss a puff from their fifteen-minute smoke break.

I wander off in another direction, down another corridor. I go to the library, not for a reading break, but just to be amongst books. Prison, in its simplest terms, is about not giving up, and not giving up requires respite.

The library here, fittingly, used to be the chapel. Taped to the double glass doors is a "Take One" folder filled with photocopies of the daily crossword. I don't take one, but a friend of mine, an avid puzzler, wrote to tell me I was last week's answer to "17 Down". Another high point, my life reduced to a clue in a crossword.

I feel safe in the library, away from the grind of the joint, away from those who invent crossword puzzles for the outside world. In here, between the green metal shelves stacked seven-feet high, are my touchstones, the rows upon rows of books.

In the old days a prison library was more likely to resemble a second-hand bookstore after a crowd of shoplifters had passed through. Now, with yearly budgets to buy the books and a television in every cell to ensure no one is interested in checking any out, the library remains well-stocked.

I move through the familiar territory, my fingers tracing the lines of books, their titles, their authors, their publishing houses. I can almost feel the whole and complete world that is inside each.

At the end of the row, I almost bump into a biker with a ponytail. His right hand, the one with the letters for L-O-V-E tattooed across the knuckles, is wrapped around a slim volume of poetry. I want to ask who he is reading. I want to ask about his left hand, which has only two letters across the knuckles — H-A. Is it a zen riddle, or a tattoo interrupted? But the guy goes two and change without the ponytail; he leaves with his poetry and my questions untendered.

Alone, I roam some more. The arrangement of this library oddly reflects the prevalent social order. Brown leather-bound law books, imposing by size and nature, sit all statesmen-like along one wall as if they were a private men's club. They even have their own sign, "Do Not Remove" as if someone is afraid we might take the law into our own hands. The adjacent wall houses the business section, beginning with a large grey tome on bank mergers, which towers above all the rest. Then management books run in descending order all the way down to small entrepreneurs. The business section breaks nicely into vacation and recreation, books on golfing, skiing, and yachting. Then we enter the trade person's section with titles on plumbing, welding, auto mechanics, and carpentry. There are no children's books in prison.

The fiction wall has the most titles, lies and escapes being favoured pastimes in here. Fiction begins with hardcovers — the classics, the new releases — but soon gives way to the gritty, the hard-boiled, the dog-eared detective paperbacks. It is in this seedier neighbourhood, the haunt of characters of Crumley and Chandler, Burke, Vacchs, and Bunker, where I am most at home.

But today I gravitate towards what booksellers in the free world would refer to as the "Woo Woo Section". In a bookstore this section would be chock-a-block with books on crystals, and candles, and Angels; guides for the twelve different stairways to heaven, recipes for dharma cookies, and chicken soup for everyone, even the chickens. You could find forgiveness, fight forgetfulness, or sue for false memory syndrome; learn to better raise your kids, your dogs, or your self-esteem. Recover your inner child, your authentic self, your femininity your masculinity, your creativity, your sexuality, or even your virginity. But back in this library, the budget for spirituality seems thinner than a ghost. There are 100 books, from Dewey Decimal 200.01 to 299.05, and fifty of them have Jesus in the title. Nowhere is innocence more lost than in the lives of those who reside here, yet the regional librarian must believe the only road to recovery is lit by the Star of Bethlehem.

A friend sent me a book, *When Things Fall Apart* written by a Buddhist nun named Pema Chödrön. Although Jesus and Buddha teach the same lesson — to learn to live with compassion for all things, I am compelled toward the Buddhist approach. Which is why I am standing here in the Woo Woo Section looking for more of Pema Chödrön. But what I find, placed there I'm sure without a trace of irony, are titles like *Break Out* or *Should I Leave?*

The title of *Life, How to Survive It* takes on new meaning if you're doing it, as does *Lethal Lovers* or *Death in the Family* if perhaps you are the cause of such books to be written. I pick out one book called *I Don't want to Be Alone* and on my way out place it on the cart that goes down to the solitary confinement unit.

My fifteen minutes of sane is up. Time to get back to work, tutoring South American drug lords in ESL. I'm thinking of getting L-O-V-E tattooed across the knuckles of one hand, and the words Ha Ha on the other. Or maybe I'll put "17 Down" on my butt, and if there's any ink left over, I'll tattoo teardrops at the corner of my eye, one for every book I'll never read.

Tough Guys Do So Vote (2004)

IN PRISON GYMNASIUMS AND JAIL CORRIDORS across the country inmates will be lining up to cast a ballot in this year's election. It is not the first time offenders have been allowed to vote. A small number of federal inmates voted in the 1997 General Election and before that an even smaller number participated in the 1992 Referendum (Charlottetown Accord).

The issue of voting rights for prisoners has been an on-again, off-again tangle of court petitions, appellate reversals, legislation and counter legislation, not to mention hot newspaper editorials and hotter talk show debates. What has become clear in constitutional law courts has done little to convince the Canadian public of why ballot boxes should be shuttled through the front gates into a prison.

Why allow the vote inside? It's a fair question. It could be defended with an earnest and humanitarian plea, or even argued in a logical and lawyerly way, but for anyone observing the actual process inside our prisons, the reason for giving criminals the vote becomes obvious — it may be the only interesting thing about this whole election.

At the onset of Election 2004 I was standing around on the top of G-Tier with a group of guys known in prison terms as regulars, or solids. They were rolling cigarettes and talking nonsense when someone from administration strode up and stapled the first notification to the bulletin board. Everyone crowded around, reading about how we could now vote. "Fuck them. I ain't voting. They're all a bunch of crooks anyway." It was the kind of talk you hear over formica tabletops and on Amen radio anywhere in the country, and the irony of the crook reference seemed to go unnoticed. There was a quick and general consensus — tough guys don't vote.

Down at the Native Centre a lot of the guys expressed similar sentiments for different reasons. As a result of being both aboriginal and a prisoner most felt twice removed from any stake in a federal election. They are more rooted in local or band issues. My Cree friend from Manitoba wondered aloud if Stephen Harper might be related to Elijah Harper but I told him, "Neither by blood nor inclination as far as I can tell." Others in the Native Brotherhood wanted to know if they could nominate Leonard Peltier.

By the time I made my way to the library a half dozen of the *Encyclopedia Britannica* crowd had abandoned their *Paris Match*s and *Atlantic Monthly*s and were seated around the reading table immersed in a civil exchange on the merits of the NDP versus the Greens. Within moments their polite chatter accelerated into a six-cylinder debate that grew so animated and loud they almost knocked over the chess board and drowned out CBC Radio 2.

I also made a point of dropping in on the Chapel group that evening. The cons for Christ were confused, as they so often are, by the Olde Testament platform of their kindred spirits in the Christian Right. The God they know and pray before, forgives the unlovable and loves the unforgivable. Don't the Conservatives know that Jesus was soft on crime?

Over the next few weeks, listening to the exchanges in laundry lineups or at canteen windows it becomes clear that within the prison world the Greens and the Marijuana Party are running at the same neck-and-neck pace as the Liberals and the Conservatives out there.

Then came the leaders' debate. Proportionately there were probably more people in here that watched the whole thing through than outside. Posters begin to appear, often with attached photocopies of news articles. Most inmate voters seem fairly relaxed over the accusations of scandal or of financial mismanagement. After all, art, politics, crime, it's what you get away with that counts. Prisoners begin walking the compound or sitting together in common areas talking of wasted votes, social programs and foreign policies, negative campaigning, party platforms, hidden agendas and not so hidden agendas. The understanding of the issues deepens.

Prisoners seem to be connecting, vigorously and passionately, to the human, social, and environmental aspects as the campaigns unfold. A fly on the wall might begin to suspect that these men are feeling a part of something, possibly a stake in their country, maybe even in their own futures. If their vote counts perhaps one day they too will count.

Still, a few cons remain apathetic, but comparably less than in any small town or neighbourhood. The Chapel group, even the Protestants, are now leaning towards Paul Martin and his Liberals. The Brotherhood decided that no native in this country can afford to be apolitical, so most are identifying with the outsider image of the Greens, plus they like the party's stance on the environment and treaty rights. The library crowd remains fairly solid NDP, but even they agree that Jack Layton's smile is thin, and his presence even thinner. The tough guys, especially those with a long history of meting out rough prison-yard justice, have now decided to vote because they are attracted to Stephen Harper's promises of harsh treatment for sex offenders. And the Marijuana Party has hardly been mentioned in weeks; I think it's a short term memory thing.

Whatever results on June 28, the journey in here has been worth the privilege. Prisoners have been registered to their home ridings, last-known residences, or places of arrest. Their impact on election results will be practically negligible. Not all, but the overwhelming majority of inmates in this country have not committed a crime so beyond the pale it excludes them forever. Canadians should be proud of extending voting rights to the very people who have offended against them. It is the measure of a true democracy, an expression of compassion and dignity, and some of that can't help but find its way back inside.

Born to Loose

IN THE OLD DAYS I USED TO MAKE BOOK. I had prestige — and fun. Handing out the betting slips, chasing down the odds, hiding it all from the guards. But write a book? After fouteen years as a cell-block gangster the only respect I get now is from a skinny embezzler who spends all his time in the Russian novelist section of the library. Just the sort of ally I need when I'm trying to convince four young turks not to borrow my television set.

My first taste of literary success came at mail call. A letter from the editor of a small magazine congratulating me on winning their poetry prize. A cheque for sixty dollars was enclosed. Sixty dollars! For my vision! My light! The reward seemed downright criminal — on the other hand sixty beans would keep me in Cheetos and Dr. Pepper's for a month.

To add insult to poet's wages, the editor had put in a P.S. "As a fellow writer I envy you the peace and solitude to pursue your chosen craft."

Peace? Solitude? Didn't this guy know that when you close a cell door the flies can still get in? Maybe he thinks those convicts hanging over the range are hollering in sign language. Give me a break! Writing in prison is like trying to juggle chainsaws during Chinese rush hour.

For every hundred guys making noises there are at least another hundred that think I'm their private writer-in-residence. Every cell has a story; every prisoner has a letter begging to be written. It gets busy. I must be the only convict in the world doing twenty-one charlies who doesn't have enough time.

I had to come up with a way to be fair so I listed all the requests in order of urgency. If a guy was over six-feet tall and could deadlift 400 pounds, it was urgent. If he was under 140 pounds, I wouldn't write him a suicide note.

Meat, for instance, my latest cell partner, asked me to pen a love poem for his girl. "You know, full of passion and stuff, like Harold Robbins." Meat keeps a knife in his sock and his brains wrapped in a bandana. I wrote:

Dear Mona,

Roses are dead

Violets are doomed

As will be you

If you don't visit soon.

Meat liked it, but wanted to add "and bring lots of drugs." Instead of a discussion on iambic pentameters and the poetic interruption of the fifth line, I reminded him he'd "only just met the girl once" and that he maybe shouldn't be so forward.

Between winning sixty-dollar poetry contests and wooing Mona, I managed to type out the two favourite words of any novelist — The End. I rushed right down to the mailroom where it cost me a month's wages to double certify and triple register my Pulitzer Prize-winning blockbuster to a top New York agency. Two months later I got the manuscript back with a note: "Great story — wrong decade. Sorry." It seemed the market for bad guys was down.

It took a further two months and a half a dozen more rejections before I signed on with a bottom New York agency. Her office was a Volkswagen camper up on blocks. I had to write back care of a licence plate in Newark.

Still, she was a New York agent — well, a New Jersey agent, but close enough. It wouldn't be long before I was being feted at one of those literary parties, sipping the bubbly and eating little weenies off toothpicks. Moguls would line up to buy my soul. Women would ask to touch my scars.

My Jersey agent got me a contract. The advance was six figures if you overlooked the decimal. With her end she bought wheels for her camper and moved to New York. We were on a roll.

I was assigned an editor. Her first letter was like a dentist's promise. She stroked me for three pages and wound up by saying, "there's some work to be done; it won't hurt a bit."

It hurt a lot. Near the end I wrote to her wondering if anyone else in the world spent two hours splaying their brains over whether to replace the word "and" with a comma. She wrote back saying "writing is war." I had been at war all my life; I had hoped writing would be different.

Finally when we had all of my participles redangled and infinitives unsplit, the lawyers moved in. They slashed and burned anything that resembled libel, truth, or an interesting sentence. The smoking remains were typeset into galleys. But when my publisher told me how many copies were being released, I said there were Italian wedding invitations that had bigger print runs.

I got an invitation to my own launch and couldn't go. My story was between covers but I was still behind bars. The parole board, instead of tripping over themselves to cut loose this literary lion, said I lacked insight. There were higher ideals at stake, they told me. I left the hearing with another year to think of some.

Meat was waiting in the hall. His lip hung when he learned I didn't make my ticket. But his mood brightened at mail call; he got a postcard from Mona. She was threatening to visit. To impress her he went to get a new tattoo.

I used the time to jot down a few ideas for a new book, which I'd begin as soon as the warden returned my typewriter. He had all the typewriters arrested last week after some serial killer had used one to start a fraudulent chain letter.

At lockdown, Meat flexed his bicep so I could read his new tack, BORN TO LOOSE, as I lay there wondering how to do another year. Hell, I could do it in a shoebox — it was enough time to get a first draft on a second novel. Of course, it might take a bit longer, writing with a seagull feather and transmission fluid, if the warden didn't give back the typewriters.

"Born to loose"? Sometimes it just works out that way.

The Art of Dying in Prison

Without My Daughter

As my daughter dives deeper into the whirlpool of her teenage years I often kid her that I must be the envy of other fathers. I am in prison and the razor wire keeps me safe. Under the watchful eyes of visiting room guards, our black humour is what we share best.

I have not been in the natural presence of my daughter since she was ten years old. We talk on the phone, write letters; our time in visits seems all too fleeting, never long enough to get down to the ground of what really hurts her out there in the real world. Sitting at right angles under revolving cameras is too strained and artificial a setting in which to untangle the confusion and conflicts. We have our occasional heart to heart but mostly we make small talk, an unacknowledged pact not to disturb much below the surface. Sophie knows, with the clarity of a fourteen-year-old, that I can only go to those places where she lives in the abstract. I see how fiercely she wants to shield me from her burdens: it is her way of loving me now, protecting me as if I were the child.

I was in the delivery room when she emerged into this world, saw how wide her liquid eyes opened for the first time. That morning an unbreakable filament of love connected us forever.

In the ensuing months I warmed her formulas and mashed her carrots. I changed a thousand nappies. I watched her learn to crawl, then stand for the first time. I heard the first words she ever uttered: "More!" I pushed her in strollers, dozed with her glued to my chest like a pygmy tree frog, and buckled her into car seats to take her everywhere I went.

I read *Goodnight Moon* until she knew where to spy the mouse on each page. We teeter-tottered in every park. We survived the stages where she wouldn't be caught wearing clothes in public, where it was lullabies on demand until I fell into a dreamy sleep beside her, and her obsession with hog-tying her nanny to the patio chairs.

I slid coins from the tooth fairy under her pillow, hid chocolate bunnies in the garden at Easter, drank the brandy and ate the Mediterranean dip she left every Christmas Eve for Santa. I drove to swim lessons and jazz-tap and ballet classes, patched bicycle tires, placed kisses on her bruises and bandages on her knees, slept beside her when she was sick, on a cot in the Children's Hospital. I piggybacked her through rain forests, built her a castle in the sand on Haida Gwaii, and built her an even bigger one when the first washed away. When my daughter grew older we fished our quota of dorado in Mexico and waltzed in a Cuban ballroom during a wild lightning storm.

Ever since I can remember Sophie has made me cards for Father's Day. She decorated them with buttons, tiny seashells, or bits of macaroni painted in splashy colours. Now that she is older she has dispensed with the decorations, but the cards haven't stopped and the messages inside haven't changed. We remain bound to one another in as primal a way as any parent and child, by our experiences, our love, and our DNA.

In 1999, the dragon that has haunted my entire life reared its fearsome head again. Within months I was living with a monster heroin and cocaine habit. Crazed and desperate, seeing no way out, I lit my life on fire. I harbour no romantic notions of what took place, only the sad admission that I robbed a bank and shot at a motorcycle cop, barely missing a woman bystander. Of all the people harmed that day Sophie remains my most enduring reminder of an innocent victim.

The day after my arrest my wife found Sophie in her room absorbed in crafting a Father's Day card, as if by this deliberate act she could bring everything back to the way it had been. But before she finished she looked up at her mother and cried, "He's not coming home is he?" Then threw herself on the bed, and sobbed her grief away.

We are about to observe our eighth straight Father's Day in prison. When I first told Sophie I would be eligible for parole on her graduation day, she seemed consoled. Then I realized she thought I meant graduation that year, which was less than three weeks away. Sophie was in Grade five, and high school must have been unimaginable.

Early in my bit I pondered the idea of taking myself off the count. A psychiatrist, one for whom I have a great deal of respect, was conducting a pretrial assessment, and saw through to my private thoughts. "This isn't about you anymore," he told me. "You've had your life, you're going to prison for a long time. This is about a ten-year-old girl. You have to show her that no matter how badly you screw up your life, you can survive, maybe even find redemption. That is the one gift you have left to give."

I began to lay a lot of hard bricks, to rise out of my addiction, up from that pit where only the self matters. I started to reclaim the heart-place of a parent, re-entered the realm of selflessness in the small and ordinary ways.

There are days when the memory of those little button and macaroni cards fill me with a terrible caring and I am overwhelmed with the numbing regret of it all. Then my name is called for a visit. Though Sophie has learned to live with the fact her life has been diminished in some ways, her love is relentless: it jumps over the razor wire. I go back to my cell, lifted by the knowledge that everything she needs is already there inside her.

The Art of Dying in Prison

His last letter was less than half a page — a small piece of yellow paper, more of a Post-it note, really. The hand-written words closed in on themselves the way his life was closing in on him now. He was weakened as much from his knowledge of the inevitable as from the disease.

I longed for his letters of old, those bulging envelopes, fifteen and twenty page raves on anything from "the amazing salad bar here at Leavenworth" to the joys of "running an eight-minute mile! Before chow line!"

After the diagnosis he wrote heroically, about beating this thing, how he was responding to the chemo, but every passing month the envelopes grew thinner. Then they became more infrequent. It was as if he were slipping away from me one page at a time. In this, his final kite before falling into a coma, the grit, even the imagination, was gone from him. He knew he wasn't going to throw some knotted sheets over the wall or tunnel his way out of this one. The letter ended with, "We've had a life haven't we. God bless. Your friend . . . , "

~~~

The first time I laid eyes on him I was young, just turned three times seven, and was holed up in a basement suite in Ottawa fresh off a prison break. The unofficial mayor of the local underworld had come to take the measure of the new kid in town. Pat's strong suit was charm and he carried it off with the smile of a little boy and the manicured look of a Las Vegas pit boss. When he peeled me off some "pocket money" from a thick roll of hundreds I knew then and there that this was a guy I wanted to get busy with. When he mentioned a "piece of work you might be interested in" I leapt at the offer.

Pat introduced me to the big leagues. Within months we had robbed millions in cash, jewellery, and gold bullion. He was usually having tea with his mother or driving his son to hockey games while I was doing the robberies. Our m.o. was established. Pat planned and I carried out the work. It was a perfect arrangement. Like Jack Spratt and his wife we licked a lot of platters clean.

Over the years we became known as The Stopwatch Gang, outlaws and fugitives. We robbed banks and armoured cars from Ottawa to San Diego to St Petersburg and back again. Later, there were others who entered into the crew with names like Skywalker, French Danny and French Gilles, The Iceman, and chiefly a little fellow named The Ghost. These were guys, with the exception of The Ghost, who parachuted in for a particular score, then left again. But Pat and I remained together. Between the two of us we have notched seven escapes, robbed hundreds of banks, and served sentences so long they looked like telephone numbers.

Throughout, we have remained bonded by deed, consequence, nature, and friendship. His last letter, which left North Carolina in a canvas mailbag marked US Bureau of Prisons, arrived in a canvas mail bag stamped Canada Corrections. Our friendship, often separated by iron bars, always found its way through the spaces between.

I'm not sure if anyone can truly know another human being but I knew Pat in ways that friends, girlfriends, priests, policemen, cell mates, bosses, even brothers, sisters, wives, or children, never could.

Pat was a man of a thousand-and-one faces. A natural-born con artist, he possessed an uncanny ability to sense whatever he, or you, needed him to be. I've watched him take a name off a tombstone and breathe life back into the long-buried deceased. He didn't just assume the guy's driver's licence and social security number, he exhumed the persona. Pat could invent a history, then inhabit an alias so consistently that it became somehow more real than the flesh. Yet, in all the roles he played, he never lost who he was in the act of who he wasn't.

As prisoners, we put on masks for the same reason people put on survival suits. As fugitives, we changed identities the way most people change their socks. New town, new history, new habits, values, and beliefs. Because I helped to guild the puppet personas I got to know the man behind the strings.

I knew Pat when he smoked cigars and heaped sour cream on his baked potato. I knew him when he ate raw carrots and ran five miles a day. I knew him as a Democrat and as a Republican, as Catholic, agnostic and Southern Methodist. I knew him when he liked black people and I knew him when he pretended not to; when he wore white shoes and pressed the pedal to the metal of a beige Cadillac, or when he wore horn rimmed glasses and drove a Volvo station wagon under the posted speed limit

Somewhere up the middle of all our tomfoolery a truth ran through that emerged time and again, despite our well-constructed roles. We were human. There were contradictions. I got to see Pat when he was kind and generous and humble to circumstance. I've witnessed him being churlish and insufferable. I've seen him act bravely and heroically, and I've looked on sadly when his nerve failed him. I've known him selfless as a monk and selfish as a two-year-old; honourable and less than honourable. He has been disingenuous to my face and honest behind my back. He has demonstrated a loyalty beyond the capacity of most human beings, yet betrayed me in the most petty of ways.

The only reason any of these things even bear saying now is that Pat saw those facets of me, too. Disappointment, as much as loyalty, defined our friendship. He went on being my friend. He punctured the piety of my expectations. He taught me that friendship is not built from ideals. Most relationships in the underworld, although at times intensely sentimental, seldom go deeper than camaraderie. Maybe it was because our lives were played in such high dramatic notes that there was no time for judgement and sourness to congeal. Perhaps because our lives depended so much, and so often, on instinct and intuition we were less dependent upon the construct of personality. Or maybe it was just our sense of heehaw, laughing at ourselves above all else. Whatever the reasons, our relationship endured and deepened, sometimes because of, sometimes in spite of, ourselves.

In the beginning Pat was my mentor. He taught me about good wine, musicals, and how not to think in nickels and dimes. By the time I was thirty, and Pat thirty-eight, he was as much student as teacher. I taught him the joys of cocaine, the language of poets, and some on-the-job training — how to throw his first bank up in the air.

In those years we may as well have been Siamese twins. Shoulder to shoulder coming out of the same bank, seated side by side in the same cars and planes as we crisscrossed the atlas. We holed up in the same apartment after every score. He rolled the enchiladas while I tossed the salad. We shared chateaubriand in hotel dining rooms and lived together in rented houses far away from the action. We borrowed each other's ties, double-dated, and drank whisky from the same bottle on the edge of a cliff in San Diego. In prison we have been cellies or lived on the same range, even played on the same hockey team. In a tight spot we'd double-team our opponents. Once, after a failed escape bid, we were cuffed, waist chained, and shackled together in the same cell in the hole. One steel bed. Only the food slot opened twice a day for eight days straight. We had to eat, stand, roll over in rhythm. We almost held hands as we took turns at the toilet.

We were competitive as race cars. We sat for years on the floor of a cellblock playing Scrabble through the bars. My word skills frustrated him but he always took the win with a more clever board strategy. Later in life I wrote a book and later still, when he began to write, I encouraged and helped edit his work. But when he published a series of articles in the newspaper and I felt demeaned by some of what he wrote I fired off a scathing review. My words danced around his on the page in a way a Scrabble board would never permit. It was our only public spat and our friendship, as always, found a way through.

More than any other way, I knew Pat through the intimacy of risk. The stakes were high when we sawed our way through bars or robbed banks with stopwatches around our necks. Time was on hold when we bluffed our way across borders or held our breath passing through roadblocks.

Pat had once, after making a clean getaway, returned through buckshot and hot lead to take me out of a very dicey spot in the parking lot of a big city mall. Another time I dressed up as a surgeon and threw down on four guards, to bust him out of a prison ambulance.

Blessed or damned, we shared a long contract with loss. Arrest was as inevitable as death and, in fact, a small death of its own. We had a throwaway phrase, that prison was "just an occupational hazard", but in the privacy of our thoughts we both knew it was the house of losers. Freshly recaptured, we would sit on opposite benches in the back of a caged van, smiling weakly at one another across the dim space, waiting for the jaws of the penitentiary to swallow us once more.

~·~·~

On January 14th, 2007, Patrick (Paddy) Mitchell died in prison in Butner, North Carolina. There was no one there to fluff his pillow or hold his hand. No family or friends, no flowers at his bedside. No witness to his final breath. Pat died alone, locked in a cell, far away from everything and everyone he knew and loved, even the country he called home.

I remember the words simply drifting through me. "Paddy died yesterday." Words I had been expecting, yet the freight they carried felt as heavy as the train they came in on. One disembodied telephone call, three words, and he was gone.

I hung up the phone, walked out of the community building, past the sounds of washers and dryers, background conversation, and the click of pool balls over on the corner table. Life moving on around me in the ordinary ways of a prison evening.

I must have cut through C Unit and crossed the darkened yard, because I found myself sitting on a stump out back of the carving shed. I stared across the black and hammered surface of the sea and let it sink in. The news drifted through me and, like fine particles of falling dust accumulating on a phantom outline, gradually made visible what was formerly unseen. The shape of death became as distinct as the engraved granite on a headstone — the moment we are born the end date is in the mail. I sagged a bit and stared into nothingness. The second-to-hardest part was knowing that there was not a damned thing that could undo Pat's dying. The hardest part was sitting there in the shadows, reminding myself to keep my back straight. Sorrow is a softening, not something to display in front of other prisoners. Truth was I didn't feel any teeth gnashing, breast beating kind of grief. I felt more numb, bereft of something. Our relationship had defined so much of my adult life, of his, of our mutual identities. Did the concept, the idea, of "us" die also? Where did his memories go? It felt as if the part of me that had joined with Pat in that long-ago basement suite in Ottawa had ended the moment his heart had stopped beating.

I have grown old in prison and seen more than my share of death, but Pat's death brought with it the absence of possibility, the end of the way I lived my life.

I'm not sure I even know grief, or the anguish of it. I have felt everything from deep sorrow to an almost total indifference towards death. Being behind bars for so much of my life has taught me that everything is bearable, that sorrow must be kept close, buried in the secret garden.

My mother, then my father, have both passed during my current sentence. For each I felt shock, then an ache, the sorrow and loss, the emptiness of a world without them in it. Only the intensity of sorrow has changed. They were my parents. I have never stopped loving them and I will never stop missing them.

I have had friends and peers and a little brother die, some of natural causes, some accidentally, and some needlessly and violently.

I learned early and well what sorrow exposes you to in the carceral world. In 1966, in Oakalla prison I was taken to the solitary confinement cells below the old cow barns for something I didn't do. It was Christmas Eve and I was all of sixteen years old and naked, save for a quilted "baby doll" gown that stopped about mid-thigh. A guard opened my door slot late that night and what he saw was a kid with his knees drawn to his chest sobbing his face off. What I saw when I looked up were the eyes of an avuncular old man, maybe a chance for sympathy or even an open door. What I got was, "Boo effen hoo." Then my slot slammed shut like a shot down the hallway and the guard announced to the rest of the guys in the hole, "This kid down here is crying." The ridicule and abuse lasted until I made bail in mid-January.

There is an eternal grief in the nature of prison life, along with an unwritten law that we must not dump more on the landscape. Like men in times of war we cannot afford to sing the songs that may weaken us. Even the language of prison forbids it. A person caught crying is "bitching up" or "sucker stroking". A teardrop tattooed under the eye signifies that a guy is doing a ten-year bid. Pat, who had fifty years in the States and twenty left from his last escape in Canada, could have tattooed five tears falling from one eye and two under the other. He didn't, but as he said in one of his near-to-last letters, "At least I'll cheat them out of watching all seven drop."

So we were defiant, survivors, but Pat and I never lost our humanity. There were times, though, in the American jungles of maximum security, where we had to set aside some of what does make us human. I remember making chit-chat about the weather with a guy as we waited for the gates to the big yard to open. There were half-a-dozen men out there with homemade knives waiting to put Xs on his eyes. He had broken the rules. If I had tipped him off to the play they'd have buried me alongside him. In the heat of the jungle you can sweat but you can't cry.

I was walking a max joint on the mainland of BC the day I was paged over the loudspeakers, told to report to the chaplain's office. I was informed that my mother had died. I recall later that day standing in the chow line, face numb, eyes set straight ahead. The guards were leaning against the far wall, weighing me up. They knew my news; it would have been sent in an earlier Observations Notice to all staff. I carried my tray to the table and chewed mechanically until the food was all gone. To show a crack in the armour, to give a face of grief to the guards lined up along the wall would be a way of sharing. I had to play a hand of solitaire; my mother didn't belong to any of this.

My case management officer informed me that I was eligible for a leave of compassion to attend her service. I was tempted to go. The funeral might give me some solace, the permission to grieve openly. I might see something, a sobbing aunt or the courage in my father's face, or hear a cousin's joke, something that would touch me, connect me communally; make me not so alone, so unsure of what to do. Then I was told I would have to go under escort with two guards and I would be wearing leg irons. I chose to stay in my cell, to participate in the rituals of bereavement through memory and my most familiar companion, imagination. I conjured up old man McNalley wearing his grey, felt gloves, driving his black hearse that would carry my mom over to the little red brick United Church on Imperial Street. My five sisters, in dark muted dresses, supporting one another. My two brothers, uncomfortable in suits, directing the traffic of mourners towards their pews. Most of the citizens of our small town would gather later in the graveyard under the whispering pines. Our family would stand nearest the damp mound of earth, the clean rectangular edges of the freshly dug hole, my father leaning on his cane and probably on one of my brothers, Mom's casket being lowered, a handful of dirt, and another.

The leg irons alone would have kept me from going, but there was another complication. I was estranged from my brothers and sisters at the time of Mom's death. They had phoned the prison chaplain, asking him to let me know. They were stingy with details. I was being punished for not being there for Mom when she was alive, for all the times I had let her down. In their consensus I had lost the right to be a part of their mourning for her. I accepted their anger; there was no one to argue with but myself. I loved my mom as much as any of them but I had to live with the consequences of my actions. I gathered up what scraps of dignity I could and laid shame atop of sadness. I let them sink down to that place where those things go to exist, the place where we don't hold grief, it holds us.

A few years after my mother passed and I was still in prison, I was called to the phone. My brother told me that our dad wouldn't be coming out of the hospital this time. A week later he died. I wrote my brother to thank him for that courtesy. When we were both quite young, whenever we fell down, banged an elbow or scraped a knee, we each, with all the fierce determination of little boys, tried hard for Dad not to see us cry. Which in a way was curious, because if tears did spring forth as they sometimes would, Dad was never harsh about it. But for me I think I would have done anything, bit clear through my lip, pinched the flesh until it was black and blue, anything other than having to make him look away. My father, born in the thirties, brought up in a working-class family, was silent, wounded by war. Like too many men of his generation, imprisoned by circumstance, he was deeply afraid of tears.

〜〜〜

I've read books and essays, texts on loss, and I've wondered why philosophers and holy men often anguished so much over the purity of their grief. All grief is pure; all grief is self-serving

Coast Salish women will sit in a darkened room, long before the sun rises and the household stirs and collect their tears in a bowl. Once the day breaks they won't be seen crying. This is to allow the spirit they are mourning to pass over to the other side, not to be held back by the sorrow of the living. I have kept my grief in a darkened room too, but for much less noble reasons. In doing so I fear I have become in some ways less of a person.

But Pat's dying changed the way I saw death, and that in turn changed the way I held grief. For the first few weeks I walked the big track every night, kicking stones. I could feel the familiar loss, but there was the odd, inexplicable flash of dread, too, as if something was wrong, and then I would really remember.

Other times I would cloud over with anger and indignation that Pat had to die in that place, that sick as my friend was, Stockwell Day, Justice Minister, would not sign his transfer papers and allow him to return to a Canadian prison via the Prisoner Exchange Treaty. He could have been visited by family during his final days. But were those feelings anything more than a way of invoking pity for him, along with a dose of self-pity, a sentiment we both hated?

When Pat was first scheduled for surgery and there was still hope, he was transferred to the federal medical facility in Butner, North Carolina. I suspect that even then he carried a homemade handcuff key under his tongue as he passed through the gates of what would prove to be his final penitentiary.

He was also looking forward to his son Kevin coming down from Canada for a visit. Kevin kept his promise, appearing with his two sons. It was the first time Pat was able to see his grandchildren. They were allowed two, two-hour visits on two consecutive days. Pat was shackled to the bed throughout and four guards stayed in the room. Kevin wrote later that Pat never uttered a word of complaint about pain or circumstance. "But Dad has never complained, has he Stevie?" No he hasn't, not in a lifetime of it. Kevin had to return to Canada with his sons, the surgery was ultimately unsuccessful, and Pat was alone with his imminent end.

Pat and I shared a life so intertwined that his death seemed to open a way for me to reconcile with the inevitability of my own dying. It became possible for me to hold my gaze on the end of life.

Through Pat, I became curious about how it all ends but stayed just one step back of letting this persuade me — through the shared bad habit of all gods and religions — towards romanticizing my notion of his, or even my own death

It took a long time for me to see his dying in that place clearly, but finally it made an almost poetic sense. His death was honest to his life, completely unsentimental. In a barren cell, uncluttered by comfort or distraction, he had to lie there on his back and stare up at a concrete ceiling. There was no dodge, no escape, no new identity to slip into. The only tombstone in the room had his own name on it.

"We've had a life haven't we." No more tunnels, no more banks, and no more letters. It wasn't a question, it was his way of introducing me to the end.

Epilogue

(*The Beachcomber*)

A FEW DAYS EACH YEAR, in the fiercest storms and the highest tides, the sea will give up messages from the past, the long-forgotten artifacts of the depths. There has been a rotted plank with the encrusted plaque from an old sailing ship, the rusted remains of a cooking pot, the occasional shard of pottery with faded Chinese characters. At the turn of the last century the immigrant ships from Europe and Asia anchored here in the big bay to unload the smallpox victims or those with leprosy. This place was a quarantine station long before it became another kind of prison. There is a graveyard on the southern side, the final resting place of those travellers who never quite made the last leg of their journey to the New World. Their graves are marked with a name, a date, and the name of the ship they sailed in on — like the one I often go to sit by: Liza Gentel, 1901–1911, *Empress of Russia*.

There are also prisoners here who, like Papillon on Devil's Island, sit and contemplate the tides, not for what they bring in, but for how fast and far they will carry something out. It is common knowledge how treacherously cold the waters that surround us are. An average-sized man will last only eight minutes before the rate of body heat loss accelerates to the point of hypothermia, followed by loss of limb function, then death.

Men have greased their bodies from head to toe with lard stolen from the kitchen and then slipped into the inky darkness, never to be heard from again. One year the prisoners staged the play *Count Dracula* for the guards and their families — after the show the lead paddled to freedom in the specially built coffin. Those left behind try to maintain the illusion that those who disappeared were successful in their attempts, but everyone knows, in the bottom of his convict heart, that for most, if not all, it was a final escape.

A pre-op tranny, Trinket, and her soon to be released boyfriend arranged a rendezvous off the point. The boyfriend got out and, at the prearranged time, Trinket dog-paddled out to meet him in his powerboat. Trinket didn't have the strength to pull herself out of the water and the splashing and commotion alerted the guards. The boyfriend panicked and gunned the outboard motor. The propellers caught Trinket, though she somehow managed to clamber aboard. She was found dead the next day by a motel chambermaid — the bed a bloody mess from her stomach having been churned open by the blades.

A one-legged friend of mine fashioned a wetsuit out of polyure-thane bags, string, and duct tape. After dark, on his big night, Ian hobbled down the rocks, unstrapped his leg, climbed into his makeshift suit and jumped in. He planned to swim to the nearest beach, half a mile across the bay, where his getaway vehicle would await. Ian told me he had been a good swimmer in high school, before the motorcycle accident. He seemed so determined and confident I didn't have the heart to give him the obvious news — that he was one leg lighter and twenty years older.

At about fifteen minutes to the 10:00 PM count I was lying on my bunk on the second floor of the dormitory wing saying prayers for Ian, when I heard my name being called from the ground below.

Ian wanted a towel and some dry clothes so he could slip in past the guards in time for count. Turned out his getaway vehicle hadn't shown up, and with one leg and a twenty-mile trek to the nearest lights, he'd turned around and swum back. We retrieved his wooden leg from the rocks the next morning. Ian finished his bit, was released, and died the same day from an overdose.

~·~·~

The years have passed and I have watched the tides come and go, carrying their debris, real and imagined. I have grown old in prison and I am only interested in beginnings these days, but the string becomes harder and harder to find. It seems I am losing the plot of my own life.

There is one trail, though, a footpath that wends its way down to a patch of grass, bordered by a flower bed and two driftwood benches. In the warm days of summer I shared this space sometimes with the occasional prisoner — a copy of Kahlil Gibran or Carlos Castaneda tucked under his arm, he came here to commit philosophy.

But the subtle varnish of autumn has given way to the songs of winter, and the philosophers are all indoors watching television. The garden is empty today, and above me the bare branches of an old Garry oak claw the sky in wild precision.

Back in October when I was tidying the place, raking the leaves, deadheading the last of the flowers, the tines of my rake caught on something heavy, half buried under the matted grass. A small dirt-and-rust-encrusted crowbar. With the heft of it in my palm I realized how it must have come to be here. Directly across the cove a low, squat building was half hidden in a stand of arbutus — the old disassociation cells. The last escape, several years ago, had been from that place. The wire that enclosed the small exercise yard out back must have been pried open by this very bar, smuggled in by another prisoner. The two men had slipped out the opening and entered the water below me, tossing the crowbar up on the bank.

They were both recaptured within days, but their escape — from the Hole — affected the lives of hundreds, if not thousands, of people. The institution, a medium-security facility, was redesignated minimum because no one can legally "escape" from a minimum. One hundred and fifty prisoners were transferred to the mainland; upwards of sixty guards and staff were relocated across the country. Families had to uproot, sell their houses; kids changed schools.

My first thought was to return the crowbar to its rightful place on the shadow board in the tool crib. But it had been missing for too long and besides, it would have been replaced. Like some other things in life it could not be returned. It would no longer fit.

I buried it there under the Buddha's impassive gaze. The most glorious things a prisoner can do is escape but the days of coffin boats and one-legged swimmers were gone forever. When I tamped down the earth over the instrument of that last escape, I felt good that, although there was no future, there would always be a past.

So it is — on these days when war breaks out in my heart and my only memories are those of a boy being shoved into the shadows of an old tractor shed, or trembling in the passenger seat of a car coming to a slow stop on a dark country road — that I can come down here to sit on this uneven patch of earth and cultivate a vacuum, a place of stillness and safety where nothing moves and no one gets hurt.

I sit on the hard ground of the prison and stare out at the hammered pewter surface of the sea. What lies beneath? I float out on these connections, escaping inwards. There is a moment when nothing moves. There is no wind, no faraway shore. Deep places draw me down. I sink slowly, lazily, like old grief, and finally come to rest at the bottom of the world.

Acknowledgements

These essays have appeared in *The Globe and Mail, Maclean's Magazine*, the *National Post*, the *Ottawa Citizen, Out of Bounds* (Canada's oldest continuously published prison magazine) *Playboy*, salon.com, the *Vancouver Sun, Vice*.

"Junkie" was first published in the anthology *Addicted: Notes From the Belly of the Beast*, edited by Patrick Lane and Lorna Crozier (D&M, 2001).

My thanks to my editor, Seán Virgo, without whom these essays would remain behind bars. And to Barry Palmer, who's always been there for me.

The epigraph by Johnny Cash, as imagined by Michael Blouin in *Wore Down Trust* (Pedlar Press, 2011), is reprinted here with permission by the publisher.